ANALYZING THE ISSUES

CRITICAL PERSPECTIVES ON
MEDIA BIAS

Edited by Jennifer Peters

Enslow Publishing

101 W. 23rd Street
Suite 240
New York, NY 10011
USA

enslow.com

Published in 2018 by Enslow Publishing, LLC
101 W. 23rd Street, Suite 240, New York, NY 10011

Library of Congress Cataloging-in-Publication Data

Names: Peters, Jennifer editor.
Title: Critical perspectives on media bias / edited by Jennifer Peters.
Description: New York : Enslow Publishing, 2018. | Series: Analyzing the
   issues | Includes bibliographical references and index. | Audience:
   Grades 7-12.
Identifiers: LCCN 2017011515 | ISBN 9780766091696 (library bound)
   | ISBN 9780766095601 (paperback)
Subjects: LCSH: Journalism — Objectivity — Juvenile literature. | Mass
   media — Objectivity — Juvenile literature.
Classification: LCC PN4784.O24 C75 2017 | DDC 302.23 — dc23
LC record available at https://lccn.loc.gov/2017011515

Printed in China

To Our Readers: We have done our best to make sure all website addresses
in this book were active and appropriate when we went to press. However,
the author and the publisher have no control over and assume no
liability for the material available on those websites or on any websites
they may link to. Any comments or suggestions can be sent by email to
customerservice@enslow.com.

Excerpts and articles have been reproduced with the permission of the
copyright holders.

Photo Credits: Cover stockphoto mania/Shutterstock.com; cover and
interior pages graphic elements Thaiview/Shutterstock.com (cover top,
pp. 1, 4-5), gbreezy/Shutterstock.com (magnifying glass), Ghornstern/
Shutterstock.com (additional interior pages).

CONTENTS

INTRODUCTION

For as long as news organizations have existed, they have strived to be impartial and fair, and to speak truth to power. Journalists and publishers have long worked to reveal the hidden truth and bring only the facts to their readers and viewers. And although most media organizations continue to proclaim their objectivity, more and more people are seeing bias in the outlets they've long trusted. Some people see a liberal bias across the media, others see a conservative bias, and still more see news biases based in race, gender, sexuality, or economic class. While journalists are trained to approach their reporting without emotion or favoritism, readers and viewers believe the age of a fair, balanced, and unbiased media is long over.

What makes people fear media bias? During elections, news organizations often choose to endorse candidates, leading many to believe the coverage they provide the rest of the time will favor the candidates or party the publishers support. Others fear the media is biased when it appears that an outlet has reported only one side of a story or has reported a story that they don't believe to be accurate. Still others fear that an outlet is biased if it covers stories that the reader or viewer doesn't believe to be true at all.

Media bias may not sound like a terrible problem, but as the country becomes more polarized politically and people worry about things like "fake news" and outside interference in American politics, it's important for the media to be a trusted institution. If people can't depend on their daily newspapers or nightly news to deliver the truth, it will become harder and harder for people to agree on what is true.

But how often is the media truly showing a bias? Experts, journalists, and readers rarely agree on which outlets are biased or what stories show bias. People on the right of the political spectrum may tell you that CNN and the *New York Times* show a liberal bias, while those to the left might be convinced that Fox News and Breitbart show a distinct conservative bias. But the issue isn't black and white, and it is in fact a very confusing shade of gray. However, the one thing that almost everyone can agree on is that there are specific elements that point to a subjective and biased story or outlet: interviewing only sources that confirm the journalist's initial hypothesis; offering an opinion in a news story; and failing to present all the facts or presenting the facts in a confusing or distorted fashion.

Indeed, there are as many ways for news organizations to show bias as there are news organizations in the twenty-first century. As you'll learn in the coming chapters, media outlets can show bias in the sources they work with, the angles they choose, the word choices they make, and the stories they choose to cover—or not cover. By reading the opinions of journalists, activists, media watchdogs, politicians, and the courts, you'll explore the issue of media bias in depth and will have the opportunity to conclude for yourself just how much of a problem bias is in today's media environment.

CHAPTER 1

WHAT THE EXPERTS SAY

Academics, media scholars, and pundits have spent years studying the media to best understand whether there is an inherent media bias, and if there is, what that means for the public. In recent years, as more and more outlets have sprung up thanks to the freedom of the internet, more outlets that express a bias have appeared, as have outlets that are "fake news," designed to push an agenda without reliance on facts but that appear just like standard news sites. What is this doing to the media? And can readers and viewers still rely on the news? In this chapter, you'll read articles that will discuss what media bias is and how it affects the media industry, as well as comparing the idea of truth to objectivity. You'll also read about a media outlet that is very upfront about a particular bias but believes it can be unbiased in other areas—the infamous Russia Today, or RT, network.

"UNDERSTANDING 'MEDIA BIAS,'" BY SEAN GONSALVES, FROM *COMMON DREAMS*, JUNE 17, 2008

You hear it all the time, especially during election season. "The media is biased" -- a criticism leveled from both the Right and Left.

In fact, there's a cottage industry devoted to "exposing media bias," most of which has people in the news biz rolling their eyes. And for good reason: not that media criticism is unwarranted, it's just that most of it, to put it bluntly, is oversimplified nonsense that generates more heat than light.

Perhaps the weakest aspect of pop media criticism is its lack of clarity. People talk about the media as if it were a single entity.

"The media"? Are we talking about the broadcast or print media? Are we talking about the *Colbert Report*, PBS, NPR, Fox News, the *Wall Street Journal* or the *Cape Cod Times*. Are we talking about reporters, editors, publishers, radio talk-show hosts, columnists, bloggers or TV pundits?

As *Washington Post* reporter Paul Farhi wrote in a recent issue of *American Journalism Review*, "critics often blame 'the media,' as if the sins of some are the sins of all. It's not just a bland, inexact generalization; it's a slur. The media are, of course, made up of numerous parts, many of which bear little relation to each other. Critics need to define their terms. Holding 'the media' responsible for some perceived slight is like blaming an entire ethnic or racial group for the actions of a few of its members."

Still, surveys show ever-increasing public skepticism about the traditional news media. According to survey data cited by media scholar S. Robert Lichter, two-thirds of the public thought the press was "fair" in a 1937 survey but by 1984 polls it dropped to 38 percent, while only 29 percent said the same about TV news.

Adding insult to injury, a national survey conducted by Sacred Heart University in January found that only 19.6 percent of respondents said they believed "all or most" reporting, while a larger percentage (23.9 percent) said they believed "little" or none of it. Next stop: zero credibility.

These survey results should be taken with a grain of salt, in part because, news consumers tend to overstate how closely they pay attention to news, as the Sacred Heart study indicates.

For example, the survey found that Americans described the *New York Times* and NPR as "mostly or somewhat liberal" -- about four times more often than they described those two outlets as "mostly or somewhat conservative."

"Leave aside the blunt generality inherent in this. (Is all of NPR -- from "Morning Edition" to "Car Talk" -- "mostly or somewhat liberal?") The more important (and unasked) question about this finding is its shaky foundation. Given that only small fractions of the populace read the *Times* or listen to NPR on a regular basis, how is it that so many Americans seem to know so much about the political leanings of the *Times* and NPR?" Farhi asks.

Part of this disconnect stems from the lack of actual content analysis among the general public and an over-reliance on anecdotal examples.

Take this year's primary campaign season, for example. Depending on which candidate you supported in the primaries, the universal claim is that the media was biased for/against Clinton or Obama. Yet, a study of the A sections of three agenda-setting newspapers (the *Washington Post, NY Times* and *L.A. Times*) done by researchers at Bowling Green State University paints a more nuanced portrait.

The study found Clinton and Obama received about the same number of "positive" and "negative" headlines from those papers (from Labor Day through the Super Tuesday primaries in early February). About 35 percent of the headlines for Obama were positive and 27 percent were negative. Clinton received 31 percent positive and 31 percent negative. The rest of stories were considered to be either mixed (with positive and negative elements) or neutral.

So what's the deal? Is the entire news biz soooo biased that it warrants such a profound sense of distrust among the public?

My own biased answer is: of course, there are media biases, most of which are on the institutional level; shaping the way news is gathered and delivered, regardless of individual preferences. But, the "media bias" news consumers decry doesn't manifest itself in the way most people think, especially as conceived by those who think the media is "liberal."

That's going to sound "liberally biased" to Limbaugh and O'Reilly fans but it's a bias shared by former Bush press secretary Scott McClellan.

"To this day, I'm often asked about the 'liberal media' critique," he writes in his new memoir. "My answer is always the same. It's probably true that most (journalists) are personally liberal or leftward leaning and tend to vote Democratic. But this tilt to the left has probably become less pronounced in recent years."

I would say that's an understatement.

"Everything I've seen as a White House press secretary and longtime observer of the political scene... suggests that any liberal bias actually has minimal impact on the way the American public is informed. We in the Bush administration had no difficulty in getting our messages out. If anything, the national press corps was probably too deferential to the White House," McClellan observes.

The run-up to the invasion of Iraq is the most obvious example. McClellan argues that the press were asking the wrong questions, focusing on the "march to war," instead of whether war was necessary. When it comes to Iraq, he writes, "the 'liberal media' didn't live up to its reputation. If it had, the country would have been better served."

For those of us who saw the invasion of Iraq as a war of choice and not necessity from day one, McClellan's observation is, by now, a truism. But what is interesting about his conservative view is that he takes it one step further.

"I'm inclined to believe that a liberal-oriented media in the United States should be viewed as a good thing," especially considering that the last several presidential administrations and the bulk of Congress have been "a succession of conservative/centrist leaders, either right of center or just left of center, who pursued mainstream policies designed to satisfy the vast bulk of middle-class American voters."

"Over the past forty years, there have been no flaming liberals in positions of greatest power in American politics. Under these circumstances, a generally liberal or left-leaning media can serve an important, useful role. It can stand up for the interests of people and causes that get short shrift from conservative and mainstream politicians."

Tell your right wing friends to put that in their Limbaugh pipe and smoke it.

Moving beyond the oversimplified and misleading debate about liberal/conservative media, there's a deeper problem to consider.

These seemingly intractable, polarized, news-views show no sign of abating. In fact, there's every reason to expect it to get worse. With the internet and the ability of news consumers to pick and choose what news they want to engage, I wonder how America will ever have a meaningful conversation about any national issue when we're all living in our own individual media bubbles, clinging to news that affirms our individual world view while rejecting any information that doesn't fit neatly into our political philosophy as worthlessly "biased."

That doesn't facilitate conversation. It encourages us to continue shouting past each other.

1. The author discusses early on the problem of considering "the media" as one singular organism instead of a collection of individuals. Do you think that considering "the media" as a collective instead of individuals leads to people seeing it as more biased or as less biased?

2. Do you think that certain outlets having a left-wing or right-wing bias prevents people from getting the news they need?

"THE TRUMPIFICATION OF THE US MEDIA: WHY CHASING NEWS VALUES DISTORTS POLITICS," BY STEPHEN CUSHION, FROM *THE CONVERSATION* WITH THE PARTNERSHIP OF CARDIFF UNIVERSITY, MARCH 10, 2016

Outside the US, the prospect of Donald Trump being elected president is typically met with a mixture of amusement and alarm. After all, how can a billionaire reality TV star become the most powerful leader in the world when he proposes building a giant wall to prevent Mexican immigrants coming to the US and banning all Muslims from entering the country?

But having been a visiting scholar at the University of Texas at Austin for the last two weeks, I've spent far too much of my time watching television news coverage of the election campaign. Once you switch on it's hard to avoid seeing or hearing Trump, listening to what other candidates think about Trump, or being exposed to policy issues that aren't viewed through the prism of Trump's politics. In fact, flicking between any one of the news channels there's little on offer besides election coverage —with Trump as the lead protagonist.

True, we're in the thick of the primary season, so perhaps a heightened emphasis on horse-race journalism is only to be expected. But my impressionistic observation of Trump's dominance holds true for far longer than a fortnight.

As reported in *The Economist*, between the beginning of 2015 and 26 February 2016, Trump received over 400 minutes of airtime on the ABC, NBC and CBS evening newscasts, compared to less than 100 minutes for both his main Republican opponents, Ted Cruz and Marco Rubio. Hillary Clinton and Bernie Sanders combined received less than half the coverage Trump did.

Since Trump is the clear frontrunner in the Republican race it is only right – journalists may argue – that he dominates the coverage and sets the agenda. But it is arguably a reliance on news values to determine campaign agendas that perpetuates the Trumpification of election reporting.

OUT OF CONTROL

In the UK, by contrast, broadcasters have to abide by strict "due impartiality" requirements in coverage of politics. Although sometimes misinterpreted, this does not result in major parties and candidates receiving equal airtime because the "due" allows for journalistic discretion. But, at the very least, it promotes a greater editorial sensitivity in exercising journalistic judgements about achieving "balance" and maintaining public confidence in the impartiality of broadcasters.

Since US broadcasters are not subject to such regulatory obligations, commercial news values can supersede (or trump!) any imperative to police the impartiality of how leaders and parties are reported. And that distorts coverage in favour of politicians who have mastered the art of what Frank Esser has called "self-mediatization": the ability to set the media agenda by appealing to the news values of mainstream journalists.

This is perhaps Trump's most successful campaigning strategy. From provocative speeches in campaign rallies to cheap personal attacks on his opponents during television debates, the Trumpification of politics is a perfect fit for the commercial goals of US broadcasters. In a recent Fox News television debate for Republican primary candidates, almost 17m viewers tuned in – the highest ratings received for any of the primary debates – but rather than exploring the policy positions of the remaining four candidates, most of the questions were either directed at Trump or revolved around him.

Many Republican voters seem to be selecting a businessman rather than a Washington insider as their preferred candidate. There is a genuinely huge story here: just as Democratic insurgent Bernie Sanders is relying on donations from citizens rather than big businesses, Trump's ability to self-fund and defy the party establishment is a fundamental challenge to the way US election campaigns are typically funded and directed. But while this might represent a refreshing change from previous election cycles, the media attention it's devouring comes at the expense of actually discussing what's really at stake.

POST-TRUTH

Of course, the spectacle of candidates evading policy issues or misleading voters is nothing new to contemporary politics. The 2012 US election was characterised as heralding an era of post-truth politics. But when a candidate such as Trump emerges, this so-called era of post-truth politics becomes an altogether more dangerous proposition than anything we've seen in recent years.

Clearly Trump's angry rhetoric connects with many people's anxieties about immigration and national security, but the impractical solutions he proposes need to be more thoroughly questioned, probed and challenged by journalists, rather than implicitly accepted and legitimised.

The politics of reactionary populist fear is hardly unique to the US. Many of Europe's democracies have lurched dramatically to the right as the continent's refugee crisis deepens – most recently Slovakia, where an openly neo-Nazi party now sits in parliament.

But where the US differs from most other advanced Western democracies is in the formal rules policing broadcast news coverage, which for many American voters is still their principal source of information about the election. The American approach to election reporting is shaped almost entirely by the pursuit of commercial news values, rather than a journalistic attempt to balance party perspectives and the views of competing candidates.

This doesn't mean the media is single-handedly responsible for the Trump phenomenon, which has emerged at a fraught time in an always-complicated political culture. But the US's dominant media system has had little impact on diminishing the opportunity for a politician with such contempt for policy to emerge as a credible Presidential candidate.

Relying on news values alone might sound like a reasonable and professional strategy for choosing election stories in a competitive industry, but it's far from politically neutral. Editorial priorities can help directly shape campaign agendas and delimit the range of issues that get discussed and debated. No-one wants an over-regulated or stifled broadcast media, but whatever one's political persuasion, surely exercising some degree of balance in election coverage can only be good for safeguarding democratic debate – whether in the US or elsewhere.

1. During the 2016 election, as the author notes, then-candidate Donald Trump received an exceptional amount of media coverage because of his uniqueness as a candidate. Do you think this sort of coverage qualifies as the media showing bias either for or against Trump?

2. The author notes that in some other countries, there are laws about equal airtime being given to candidates for political office. Do you think a law like this would help curb media bias in the US, or would it create more bias because outlets would feel forced to cover all candidates equally regardless of the newsworthiness?

"AMERICANS ARE TO BLAME FOR THE FRACTURED STATE OF THE MEDIA," BY CARL FORSLING, FROM *TASK & PURPOSE*, OCTOBER 16, 2016

The way we consume news enables us to only follow outlets that reinforce our existing views, and that's a big problem.

Thirty years ago, there was such a thing as "the media." The daily paper was dropped on everyone's doorstep in the morning. When dad came home from work, he'd switch on the television and watch the nightly news on one of the big three networks while waiting for dinner.

We got our news from the same places, so while people would occasionally complain about some type of bias, at least all of America was looking at generally the same content. Like the sky. Maybe it was light blue, maybe it was a pastel blue, but no one claimed the sky was green and that it was the result of a secret United Nations plot to use chemtrails to change the color.

Famously, the late Sen. Daniel Moynihan reportedly once said, "You are entitled to your own opinion, but you are not entitled to your own facts." It used to be that American society generally agreed on the facts at hand, even if their individual values and beliefs led them to draw different conclusions from those facts.

Today, though, that seems to be less of the case. Whatever version of the "facts" audiences want are available on the internet. For better or worse, anyone can establish a semi-professional-looking news website, even if his only professional qualification is having a few dollars for a domain and an axe to grind. No matter what crazy view one is already predisposed to have, one can find a "news" outlet willing to back it up. As one researcher wrote, the media has become fragmented, which ultimately feeds polarization.

Social media platforms proliferate this practice. Many people today get a substantial portion of their news exclusively from social media, specifically Facebook. Everyone "likes," "shares," and "favorites" those articles expressing points of view they agree with. Social media platforms exist to make money from keeping people's eyeballs on their sites, so they respond by giving the viewer more of the same, reinforcing existing preconceptions even more.

In the course of many discussions, civil and otherwise, I often link or quote sources that would have been unimpeachable before — stories from some of the premier news sources in American journalism, like The New York Times, The Washington Post, The Wall Street Journal, NPR, etc. All dismissed as biased. The problem with this is that all too often, "biased" just means that the news consumer doesn't like what he's being told. Even articles that are impeccably sourced are disregarded simply because they're from the "mainstream media."

By way of retort, someone will post something from a website that doesn't even make a cursory attempt at neutrality, often from online sources that solely traffic in rumors and conspiracies. The standard retort to this is usually something like "at least they acknowledge their bias." That's true, for what it's worth, which isn't much. The problem with it is that most people who point it out don't try to balance it out with views from the other side, much less try to find a more impartial source. They find a site that buttresses their beliefs and stop there.

The alternative is some type of government-operated news service like the BBC, or a reinstatement of the Fairness Doctrine — a policy abolished in 1987 that called for public broadcast license-holders to present important issues through multiple perspectives — either of which would undoubtedly elicit even worse claims of bias than the present system. It's up to news consumers themselves to reward good news outlets with their business — that's what will improve the news media, not the government or a crisis of conscience in the boardrooms of media conglomerates.

Prior to the internet, market forces worked as a pretty good check and balance. If a network or newspaper went too far astray, it lost viewers to one of its competitors, which eventually pulled it back to the middle. With the fracturing of the market into micro-targeted segments, that centering function is gone. Now viewers just leave to one of a thousand information sources each trying to generate inflammatory clickbait headlines. Whereas once the choice between news sources was Wheaties or Cheerios, today the traditional news media is trying to sell Wheaties while some of its digital competitors market Oreo cookies, and others are selling straight crystal meth.

As long as the media in this country remains free, which it should, it's the responsibility of every informed person to eat his Wheaties. If you're a citizen who considers yourself informed, whether liberal or conservative, you need to have a foundation of general news from an established news source, e.g., an organization that has actual reporters with bureaus in major cities or that at least uses major news wires like Reuters or McClatchy, not just a sketchy aggregator site. Only after that should you rely on opinion-oriented sites or sites with well-established angles on the news. You've got to eat a balanced meal before you eat dessert. Feed your mind nothing but garbage and it will become fat and lazy.

And as far as educating yourself, do yourself a favor and follow some that run counter to your own inclinations. Follow both Mother Jones and National Review, Fox News and MSNBC. It's not only a good way to fact check both sides, but it will also serve to remind you that the other ideological side isn't trying to destroy America. Most of either side sincerely wants the best for this country. They just happen to have a different perspective than you. Too many people dig into their ideological fighting holes and consume media only to throw derogatory news grenades at the other side.

Finally, for the love of all that's holy, stop clicking on conspiracy-theory sites. You're just feeding their cancer on society with your traffic and shares. You should know them when you see them. Gaudy banner headlines and words like "REVEALED!" and "EXPOSED!" in all caps should ring alarm bells in your mind.

Blaming the news media at large for the state of today's civil discourse and polarization is like blaming Taco Bell for the obesity epidemic. Sure they could do more to help, but really they're just giving the people what they want.

The solution lies in each and every one of us stop consuming junk media before it consumes us all.

1. One way the author suggests combating your exposure to news that only shows a particular bias is to receive your news from opposing outlets so that you can compare the angles and facts and reach the truth. What are other ways you can think of to make sure you're thinking critically about the news you read or watch and not blindly trusting any one particular outlet?

2. Do you think media outlets suffer any consequences for showing a blatant bias? If so, what are the consequences? If not, why do you think that is?

"DOES NONPARTISAN JOURNALISM HAVE A FUTURE?" BY JUSTIN BUCHLER, FROM *THE CONVERSATION* WITH THE PARTNERSHIP OF CASE WESTERN RESERVE UNIVERSITY, JANUARY 5, 2017

The nonpartisan model of journalism is built around the norm of covering politics as though both parties are equally guilty of all offenses. The 2016 campaign stressed that model to the breaking point with one candidate — Donald Trump — who lied at an astonishing level. Politi-Fact rates 51 percent of his statements as "false" or "pants on fire," with another 18 percent rated as "mostly false." His presidency will continue to make nonpartisan journalistic norms difficult to follow.

As a political scientist focused on game theory, I approach the media from the perspective of strategic choice. Media outlets make decisions about how to position themselves within a market and how to signal to news consumers what kinds of outlets they are in ideological terms. But they also interact strategically with politicians, who use journalists' ideological leanings and accusations of leanings to undermine the credibility of even the most valid criticisms.

While Republican politicians have decried liberal media bias for decades, none has done so as vehemently as Trump, who polarizes the media in a way that may not leave an escape.

THE DEVELOPMENT OF A NONPARTISAN PRESS

In the 20th and 21st centuries, news outlets have made their money through subscriptions, sales and advertisements. However, before these economic models developed, newspapers had a tough time turning a profit.

In the 19th century, many newspapers were produced and distributed by institutions that weren't in it for the money. Political parties, therefore, were a primary source of news. Horace Greeley's Jeffersonian — an outlet for the Whig Party — had a decidedly partisan point of view. Others, like The Bay State Democrat, had names that told you exactly what they were doing. When Henry Raymond founded The New York Times in 1851 as a somewhat more independent outlet despite his Whig and Republican affiliations, it was an anomaly. Nonetheless, partisan newspapers, for economic and political reasons, were common throughout the 19th century, particularly during the early 19th century.

The information in partisan newspapers was hardly unbiased. But nobody expected anything else because the concept of a neutral press didn't really exist. The development of a neutral press on a large scale required both a different economic production and distribution model and the recognition that there was a market for it.

The muckraking era that began in the early 20th century brought such journalism into the forefront. Muckraking, the forebear of investigative journalism, traces back to Upton Sinclair and fellow writers who uncovered corruption and scandal. Its success demonstrated demand for papers that weren't partisan, and production and distribution models developed that allowed more nonpartisan papers to turn a profit by filling a gap within the market.

The economic principles at work are always the same. There is a balancing act between the costs of entry and the size of the audience that can be reached which determines when new media outlets can form, just as in any other market. The trick is that costs and benefits change over time.

NEUTRALITY NORMS IN A COMPLEX MEDIA ENVIRONMENT

Just as market incentives supported the development of a neutral press, market incentives, combined with technology, have allowed institutions like Fox News and MSNBC to provide news coverage from decidedly conservative and liberal perspectives, with internet sources further fragmenting the media environment into narrow ideological niches.

These media outlets, though, muddy the signals: A nonpartisan journalist strives to levy valid criticism, but a partisan journalist will always criticize the opposing party. Thus a weakly informed voter will have a difficult time distinguishing between, say, a valid accusation from a nonpartisan journalist that a Republican is lying and partisan bias from a left-wing journalist who fails to acknowledge that bias.

The current media landscape is a hybrid, combining opinion-based outlets that resemble the party-affiliated newspapers of the 19th century and journalistic outlets that attempt to follow the muckraking model that developed in the 20th century. The way the latter attempt to distinguish themselves from the former is by following norms of neutrality and asserting that both parties are equally guilty of all political sins. This model breaks down when the parties are no longer equally guilty.

Consider the first presidential debate of 2016. Hillary Clinton mentioned Trump's 2012 claim that global warming was a Chinese hoax. Trump interrupted to deny having made the claim. Not only had Trump engaged in an outlandish conspiracy theory, but he also lied during a debate about having done so.

"Both sides do it" is not a valid response to this level of dishonesty because both sides do not always engage in this level of dishonesty. Yet it was relatively normal behavior for Trump, who rose to the top of the Republican Party by gradually taking leadership of the "birther" movement and eventually even tried to switch the blame for that to Clinton.

The strategic problem in this type of situation is more complex than it appears, and it is what I call "the journalist's dilemma." The nonpartisan press can let the lie go unremarked. But to do so is to enable Trump's lies. On the other hand, if they point out how much he lies, Trump can respond with accusations of liberal media bias. Trump, in fact, goes further than past Republicans, even directing crowd hostility toward specific journalists at rallies.

The media landscape, though, is populated by outlets with liberal leanings, like MSNBC, so uninformed news consumers who lack the time to do thorough investigations of every Trump and Clinton claim must decide: If a media outlet says that Trump lies more than Clinton, does that mean he is more dishonest or that the media outlet is a liberal one? The rational inference, given the media landscape, is actually the latter, making it self-defeating for the nonpartisan press to attempt to call out Trump's lies. This might explain why a plurality of voters thought that Trump was more honest than Clinton, despite a record of more dishonesty from Trump at fact-checking sites like PolitiFact.

NONPARTISAN JOURNALISM IN A TRUMP PRESIDENCY?

Is there a way for the neutral press to point out when Trump lies and not have that information get discounted as partisan bias?

The basic problem is that the norms that have guided the nonpartisan press are built around the assumption that the parties are mirror images of each other. They may disagree on policy, but they abide by the same rules. The nonpartisan press as we know it, then, cannot function when one party systematically stops abiding those norms.

The 2016 campaign was an example of what happens when the parties are out of balance. Trump simply lied far more than Clinton, but the nonpartisan press was unable to convey that information to the public because even trying to point that out violates the "both sides do it" journalistic norm, thereby signaling bias to a weakly informed but rational audience, which invalidates the criticism.

Unfortunately, then, the nonpartisan press is essentially stuck, at least until Donald Trump is out of office. While there is no longer a "he said, she said" campaign, the fact that Trump is not only the president but the head of the Republican Party makes his statements informal positions of the Republican Party. For the press to attack those statements as lies is to place themselves in opposition to the Republican Party, making them de facto Democratic partisans.

Because Trump is an entertainer rather than a policymaker, it is difficult for the press to even interview him as a normal political figure since he does not respond to facts in conventional ways. Each time he lies, any media outlet that aspires to objectivity must decide whether to point it out — which would make it indistinguishable from the Democratic-aligned press — or to allow the lie to go unremarked, thereby remaining complicit in the lie, tacitly aiding the Republican Party. Neither is likely to inform anyone in any meaningful way, which renders the model of the neutral press nearly inoperable.

1. The author suggests that during the 2016 presidential campaign, the media tried to fight accusations of bias by implying that all candidates were equally unpleasant choices. Do you think this sort of media behavior helps them fight their bias, or does it show a greater bias?

2. The author says that it's often difficult for readers to tell the difference between a partisan journalist complaining about the opposing party and a nonpartisan journalist leveling a valid complaint against someone. What are some examples of objective news stories that could appear biased to the untrained eye? How can you tell the difference?

"WHY JOURNALISTIC 'BALANCE' IS FAILING THE PUBLIC," BY BRUCE MUTSVAIRO, FROM *THE CONVERSATION* WITH THE PARTNERSHIP OF NORTHUMBRIA UNIVERSITY, NEWCASTLE, NOVEMBER 25, 2016

Renowned reporter Christiane Amanpour recently told a conference of the Committee to Protect Journalists that they should aim for truth over neutrality. Watching the recent US presidential campaign unfold, she said she was "shocked by the exceptionally high bar put before one candidate and the exceptionally low bar put before the other candidate". She went on:

> It appeared much of the media got itself into knots trying to differentiate between balance, objectivity, neutrality, and crucially, truth.

> We cannot continue the old paradigm – let's say like over global warming, where 99.9% of the empirical scientific evidence is given equal play with the tiny minority of deniers.

But surely truth is a matter of perspective — and shouldn't a journalist aim instead to report impartially and in a balanced manner? Eight years ago, Carl Bernstein —of Watergate fame — told a packed audience attending the annual Perugia International Journalism Festival that good journalism revolved around "trying to obtain the best attainable version of the truth". But in an era where news can be shipped to your phone in a matter of seconds, it's becoming increasingly difficult to distinguish truth from lies.

And even truth-seeking journalists could easily be pressured into inadvertently or even intentionally covering stories in order to satisfy a false or imaginary sense of balance. You can't blame them. The concept of "balance" — or as its critics refer to it "false equivalence" — has long been a key precept of journalism. It epitomises the idealistic notion that journalists ought to be fair to all so that, whenever they write a story, they give equal weight to both sides of the argument.

But, especially in our new "post-truth" era, this doesn't always work to the benefit of the public good. Here are some examples of where balance doesn't necessarily work.

US PRESIDENTIAL ELECTION

Supporters of Hillary Clinton are still smarting about the coverage of her email server which was used to balance out the whiff of scandal that dogged Donald Trump's campaign. Of course, Trump's supporters also bitterly complained that he was unfairly targeted by the mainstream press. But is it right to seek to balance reporting in a presidential campaign where one candidate has a question mark over her use of a private email account (something her predecessor Colin Powell has admitted to doing) and the other candidate is linked to myriad scandals, including questionable tax practises, multiple bankruptcies and sexual assault allegations (which he denies).

The pursuit of balance is impractical — but this doesn't mean journalists should pull back from investigating important stories. New York Times public editor Liz Spayd was right when she recently defended her colleagues in the wake of growing protests from readers who complained about the paper's investigations into whether countries that had made donations to the Clinton Foundation had received special treatment from Hillary Clinton's State Department (they found nothing). Spayd says that the danger of this is clear:

> Fear of false balance is a creeping threat to the role of the media because it encourages journalists to pull back from their responsibility to hold power accountable. All power, not just certain individuals, however vile they might seem.

But you can't help but have some sympathy for Jacob Weisberg of Slate magazine, quoted in Spayd's article, who said that journalists used to covering candidates who were like "apples and oranges" were presented with a candidate, Trump, who was like "rancid meat".

BREXIT

In a sense, the reporting of the EU referendum campaign was anything but balanced. A study by Loughborough academics found that — when you took newspaper circulation into account — there was a weight of 82% to 18% in favour of articles arguing the case for the Leave campaign.

Given that the majority of experts believed that leaving the European Union would adversely affect the UK economy, had their perspectives been fairly reported against the few genuine experts who supported the arguments for Leave, few would realistically have expected the eventual result.

Overreliance on balance can itself lead to unwanted bias. A study by Jeremy Burke concluded that the public suffers as a result of the fact that many media organisations, who are desperately seeking neutrality in their reporting, directly or indirectly withhold important information.

CLIMATE CHANGE

The environmental debate has provided perhaps the most egregious examples of why balance is failing journalism and the public. As Amanpour highlighted in her speech, in spite of overwhelming scientific evidence linking humans to global warming, news media eager to provide balance to the debate continue to challenge this notion.

Like everyone, journalists have every right to challenge scientific knowledge. But simply challenging it, or presenting dubious assertions for the sake of balance can skew the debate — against public interest.

Amanpour exhorted her audience to action, saying: "We must fight against normalisation of the unaccept-able." One way to do this is to recognise that this is what false balance can do. And to realise, once and for all, that it is failing journalists and their audiences.

1. Do you think journalists aiming for objectivity can actually prevent themselves from presenting the truth, as Christiane Amanpour suggests? What do you think makes "objectivity" or "truth" different from "neutrality"?

2. The author discusses "false balance," which is the idea that there are times when giving both sides of an argument equal weight implies that both sides are equally valid when they may not be. An example the author gives is climate change, which the majority of the scientific community believes to be real and caused by human influence, but that the media often tries to balance by presenting nonbelievers as having equal stake in the issue. What are other stories that could suffer from journalists offering a false balance?

"CAN A RUSSIAN-FUNDED CABLE NETWORK ACTUALLY PROMOTE FREE PRESS IN THE U.S.?" BY SOPHIA A. MCCLENNEN, FROM *THE CONVERSATION* WITH THE PARTNERSHIP OF PENNSYLVANIA STATE UNIVERSITY, MARCH 29, 2016

With the recently announced shutdown of Al Jazeera America, the alternative cable news scene is in flux.

Launched as a corrective to the politicized and spectacle-heavy programming of Fox News, CNN and MSNBC, Al Jazeera America positioned itself as a fact-based, unbiased news source. Even though the network won awards for reporting, the Qatari government-funded channel suffered from the public perception that it had an anti-Western, pro-Islamic stance. Amid lowering gas prices and reports of other financial woes, the channel announced it would shut down its U.S. operations at the end of April.

As Al Jazeera America closes shop, it's worth wondering how this change will affect the position of RT America — previously known as Russia Today America — in the U.S. market. Like Al Jazeera, RT America has fashioned itself as a serious alternative to the politicized media circus promoted by the top three cable news stations. Unlike Al Jazeera, it runs ad-free, which arguably gives it even more potential for influence-free programming.

But RT America has some inherent contradictions: it offers a "Russian state perspective" in its news programming while simultaneously airing some of the most progressive shows on U.S. cable. As Julia Ioffe writes in the *Columbia Journalism Review*, RT America often acts as a "shrill propaganda outlet" for the Kremlin — an identity that clashes with its desire to compete in the international news market.

At the same time, according to Ioffe, RT America understands that in order to effectively compete with other progressive, unbiased networks, it needs "to be taken seriously." This realization, she explains, has led to some good reporting.

It's a crazy notion — and a bit mind-boggling to consider — but RT America might be offering some of the most progressive, uncensored cable media programming in the U.S. today.

Certainly some will not be able to look past the paradox that a nation that has one of the lowest scores on the press freedom index could also be funding a valuable alternative to mainstream cable news.

But when it comes to distorting the news, is the network any more culpable than mainstream cable networks? And can U.S. audiences overcome their inherent prejudice that RT America is just a propaganda arm for the Russian government?

THE RT AMERICA PARADOX

Thus far, most coverage of RT America has focused on its ties to the Kremlin. But there's a distinct difference between the news arm of the Moscow-based Russia Today and RT America's opinion shows.

In short, the opinion and talk shows that populate RT America seem to have editorial freedom, while the news arm of RT does not.

One stark example took place over coverage of the conflict between Russia and the Ukraine.

RT news anchor Liz Wahl resigned on air, citing disagreements with RT's editorial policy. More recently, Moscow-based Sarah Firth — who worked for RT, not RT America — resigned in protest over the way that the network was covering the Malaysian Airlines crash in Ukraine.

In contrast, Abby Martin, former host of "Breaking the Set," an opinion show that aired on RT America from 2012 to 2015, openly criticized Russian military intervention into Ukraine in March of 2014. Yet she went on to continue to host her show for another year before moving on. In a note for Media Roots, she explained she was leaving the show to pursue more investigative reporting and added "RT has given me opportunities I will be eternally thankful for."

This suggests a divide at RT America over freedom of expression in opinion shows versus news coverage. It's a distinction that is important to note and to critique. But it's also one that suggests that the assumption that all RT America programming is tainted by propaganda may itself be an unfounded bias.

THE RT DIFFERENCE

While Al Jazeera America and RT America both angled to offer an alternative to mainstream U.S. news media, there are many ways that RT has followed a different — and potentially more successful — path.

First, RT America made the smart move to remove Russia from its name. Al Jazeera refused to adjust its name to appeal to U.S. viewers and distance itself from its financial backers.

RT America has also differed radically in the sort of programming offered. Balancing out its daily news programming, RT America airs analysis and commentary shows by Larry King, Thom Hartmann, Jesse Ventura and former MSNBC host Ed Schultz — all established personalities with significant appeal to American audiences.

In addition, RT America has carved out a niche with millennial viewers, with two shows aimed at a younger audience and hosted by younger talent. The first, "Watching the Hawks," is a news magazine show hosted by Tyrel Ventura (Jesse's son), Sean Stone (Oliver's son) and Tabetha Wallace.

When they were announced as new hosts for a show on RT, many dismissed the development. Wallace told me, for instance, that she is often derogatorily called "Putin's princess," since it's assumed the Russian leader controls her.

But I believe "Watching the Hawks" has fed viewers a consistent diet of cutting-edge stories on politics, media and culture. They often target corporate abuse, like pieces they've run on HSBC and Dow-Dupont.

Meanwhile, Wallace has reported on the annual gathering of veterans called "The Bikers of Rolling Thunder," and she covered the 70th Hiroshima Peace Ceremony. In my opinion, both segments are solid examples of stories that had been largely ignored in the mainstream U.S. media.

The second millennial-oriented show on RT America is "Redacted Tonight," a satirical news program hosted by political comedian Lee Camp.

Camp — described by Salon as "Jon Stewart with sharper teeth" — appeals to an audience that has become increasingly dissatisfied with mainstream news.

Since 9/11, satire news has increasingly been taken more seriously than "real" news (even though it doesn't exactly live up to that standard). Nonetheless, Jon Stewart was voted most trusted journalist after Walter Cronkite died. And viewers of "The Daily Show" and "The Colbert Report" scored higher than viewers of network news in knowledge of public issues.

Taking advantage of the fact that RT airs no advertising, Camp goes after any and all corporate and political malfeasance he can uncover. And he makes his audience laugh while doing it.

Recent episodes highlighted how the media claimed Hillary Clinton won the first Democratic debate even though Bernie Sanders won every poll, and pointed to the ongoing inability of the U.S. public to have a meaningful conversation about Israel and Palestine.

Like Jon Stewart, Lee Camp uses humor to criticize mainstream media coverage.

These sorts of shows were missing on Al Jazeera America. The network never attempted to break into the "fake news" market, despite the fact that it's a growing source of news and entertainment for young viewers. Nor did they provide the sort of hip, inquisitive programming found on "Watching the Hawks."

Arguably, these two shows could build a young base of viewers for RT America.

A NETWORK OF INDEPENDENT PERSONALITIES

While skeptics may think that these shows can't possibly be free of Kremlin influence, many of the top-billed hosts for RT America — Larry King, Jesse Ventura,

Thom Hartmann and Ed Schultz — all share a history of being independent thinkers.

Take Thom Hartmann's show, "The Big Picture." Hartmann, a radio and TV personality and author of over 25 books, has made his career as a progressive political commentator. His two writers work in RT America's Washington, D.C. studio, and they both told me that they have zero restrictions on what they cover each night.

When I asked Hartmann, he said, "No one at RT has ever told me what to say and what not to say."

Meanwhile he explained that in any given week, "The Big Picture," covers at least three stories that simply would never appear on mainstream cable news. And yet, despite the fact that "The Big Picture" also airs on the progressive cable network Free Speech TV, his presence on RT America has to contend with assumptions of censorship and control.

King has also done a series of interviews where he's had to justify his ties to the network. In each case, he has explained that he hates censorship and that his own show is completely free of any editorial control. He has also openly disagreed with Russian policies: "I certainly vehemently disagree with the position they take on homosexuals – that's absurd to me."

No one asks anchors on NBC how it feels to work for a weapons contractor. Numerous studies, including one out of the University of Michigan, have shown that the link between GE and NBC has led to biased reporting.

Not only is the U.S. media influenced by corporations; it's also influenced by the federal government.

In 2006, journalists Amy and David Goodman reported that "Under the Bush administration, at least 20 federal agencies … spent $250 million creating hundreds of fake television news segments that [were] sent to local stations." They also documented how the government paid journalists in Iraq for positive reporting, and provided canned videos to air on cable news.

Given these examples of political and corporate influence on mainstream networks, it is worth wondering why RT gets criticized for bias while other networks get a free pass.

Lee Camp says he was drawn to RT in the first place precisely because of the editorial freedom. He knew he wouldn't have to worry about pressure from advertisers.

As he explained in the opening of one episode:

People [ask] me why Redacted Tonight is on RT and not another network...I'll tell you why. My anti-consumerism, anti-two-party-corporate-total-itarianism isn't exactly welcomed with open arms on networks showing 24/7 Wal-Mart ads.

A NEW CULTURAL COLD WAR?

RT America has certainly embraced its paradoxical role of pushing media boundaries in the U.S. that likely wouldn't be tolerated on Russian soil. But before we fall into Cold War dichotomies of U.S. press freedom and Russian media censorship, it's important to note two key realities in the 21st-century media landscape.

First, while it's important to hold RT America accountable for its coverage of Russia's intervention into Ukraine, it's worth noting that the U.S. media could equally be held accountable for its own coverage of the 9/11 attacks and the lead-up to the U.S.-Iraq War.

In 2015, four out of 10 Americans still believed there were weapons of mass destruction found in Iraq — a level of disinformation that requires media compliance. These statistics show the long-lasting impact of media bias in shaping public opinion.

Furthermore, the current U.S. news media is filled not only with bias but also with outright lies. Fox News, the most-watched cable news network, lies about 60 percent of the time, according to Politifact. For NBC and MSNBC, the score isn't much better: 46 percent.

One wonders how RT America would compare.

1. Russia Today, or RT, is a Russian state–sponsored media outlet, and as such, they are essentially censored by the Russian government when it comes to news regarding Russia. However, as the article expresses, they have also done good reporting on their American channel, RT America. Do you think an outlet like this can truly offer any unbiased news to viewers? Why or why not?

2. How can viewers of RT America's talk shows ensure that they're not falling for biased reporting? What are steps they can take to make sure that, even if RT's shows are biased, they will be able to get the full story?

CHAPTER 2

WHAT THE GOVERNMENT AND POLITICIANS SAY

Those in the government are often the subjects of claims of media bias, with politicians on the left or right claiming that news outlets are biased against them because of their political party. This claim has become more common in recent years and reached an especially loud cry during the 2016 presidential election. But are politicians really affected by media bias? As you'll see in this chapter, politicians from all sides can often feel that the media is unfairly presenting their story because of a bias. But it isn't all about politics. The government has taken a stance against media bias and "fake news" in the past several years in an effort to help protect the public from false or exaggerated reporting. As you read this chapter, you'll read comments from President Trump and his staff, as well as the text of bills that were put before Congress in an effort to combat media bias, and you'll be asked to think about how much impact the government has on the media—and how much effect the media has on the government.

"HOUSE PASSES BILL TARGETING 'RUSSIAN PROPAGANDA' AND 'FAKE NEWS,'" BY WHITNEY WEBB, FROM TRUEACTIVIST.COM, DECEMBER 4, 2016

Since the US election concluded, "fake news" and "Russian propaganda" have become commonly cited by Clinton supporters and parroted by the corporate media as the scapegoat for Trump's "shocking" victory. However, as recent articles from the corporate-owned media have shown, the "Russian propaganda" and "fake news" have both become umbrella terms for a range of opinions that are critical of the US government and its policies. Now, the US government has officially intervened with the passage of HR 6393, titled the "Intelligence Authorization Act for Fiscal Year 2017." The bill, which passed on November 30, touches on several intelligence-related issues, including managing the effects of "propaganda," specifically that directly or indirectly funded in some way by Russia.

Section 501 of the bill deals specifically with countering "active measures by the Russian Federation to exert covert influence over peoples and governments." These active measures, according to the bill, include "activities intended to influence a person or government that are carried out in coordination with, or at the behest of, political leaders or the security services of the Russian Federation" even if the "role of the Russian Federation has been hidden." Among the examples of such activities are "covert broadcasting," "media manipulation," "disinformation," and "incitement."

The use of incitement is particularly interesting as this term was also used by the state of Israel to crack down on dissent on Facebook, which led to the banning of several accounts belonging to Palestinian journalists and news agencies. The term "disinformation" is also riddled with problems as the term could easily be used to censor any information that runs contrary to the government's own narrative. "Media manipulation" and "covert broadcasting" are both sufficiently broad as to include a story that the government finds to be working against its interests. According to the bill, these "active measures," whether "hidden" ties to Russia are proven or not, will be investigated and "countered" by an inter-agency committee set to include appointees of the Secretary of State, Secretary of Defense, and Secretary of the Treasury among others. This committee's main duty will be to "expose falsehoods," though the President "may designate" other relevant duties to the group.

Some corporate media outlets have already shown how this bill could be used to silent dissenting viewpoints under the guise that they are unwittingly serving Russian ends. The Washington Post recently published a piece by Craig Timberg titled "Russian propaganda effort helped spread 'fake news' during election," which cited a group of "experts" who have claimed that reputable, independent news organization such as Counterpunch, Zero Hedge, Truthdig, True Activist, and the Drudge Report among others are all part of a "sophisticated" Russian propaganda campaign.

The organization cited in the article, known as PropOrNot, has already had its credibility shredded by the New Yorker and the Intercept. However, that hasn't stopped major journalists and even politicians from sharing the Washington Post's story as a stunning exposé. The most dangerous thing about PropOrNot is that they argue that exhibiting a pattern of beliefs, including anti-interventionism and anti-GMO, is enough to risk being labeled a Russian propagandist. This organization has called for those they have placed on their "list" to be investigated by the FBI and DOJ for violations of the Espionage Act. Could this latest bill be the government's first step in following through with this suggestion?

1. After having read about media bias in chapter one, do you think a bill against Russian media manipulation will help fix the problem of media bias in America?

EXCERPT FROM "H.R. 6393 (114TH): INTELLIGENCE AUTHORIZATION ACT FOR FISCAL YEAR 2017, SECTION 501," FROM THE UNITED STATES SENATE, DECEMBER 1, 2016

TITLE V—MATTERS RELATING TO FOREIGN COUNTRIES

SEC. 501. COMMITTEE TO COUNTER ACTIVE MEASURES BY THE RUSSIAN FEDERATION TO EXERT COVERT INFLUENCE OVER PEOPLES AND GOVERNMENTS

(a) Definitions.—In this section:

(1) Active Measures by Russia to Exert Covert Influence—The term active measures by Russia to exert covert influence means activities intended to influence a

person or government that are carried out in coordination with, or at the behest of, political leaders or the security services of the Russian Federation and the role of the Russian Federation has been hidden or not acknowledged publicly, including the following:

(A) Establishment or funding of a front group.

(B) Covert broadcasting.

(C) Media manipulation.

(D) Disinformation and forgeries.

(E) Funding agents of influence.

(F) Incitement and offensive counterintelligence.

(G) Assassinations.

(H) Terrorist acts.

(2)Appropriate Committees of Congress—The term appropriate committees of Congress means—

(A) the congressional intelligence committees;

(B) the Committee on Armed Services and the Committee on Foreign Relations of the Senate; and

(C) the Committee on Armed Services and the Committee on Foreign Affairs of the House of Representatives.

(b) Establishment.—There is established within the executive branch an interagency committee to counter active measures by the Russian Federation to exert covert influence.

(c) Membership.—

(1) In General.—

(A) Appointment.—Each head of an agency or department of the United States Government set out under subparagraph (B) shall appoint one member of the committee established by subsection (b) from among officials of such agency or department who occupy a position that is required to be appointed by the President, with the advice and consent of the Senate.

(B)Head of an Agency or Department.—The head of an agency or department of the United States Government set out under this subparagraph are the following:

(i) The Director of National Intelligence.

(ii) The Secretary of State.

(iii) The Secretary of Defense.

(iv) The Secretary of the Treasury.

(v) The Attorney General.

(vi) The Secretary of Energy.

(vii) The Director of the Federal Bureau of Investigation.

(viii) The head of any other agency or department of the United States Government designated by the President for purposes of this section.

(d) Meetings.—The committee shall meet on a regular basis.

(e) Duties.—The duties of the committee established by subsection (b) shall be as follows:

(1) To counter active measures by Russia to exert covert influence, including by exposing falsehoods, agents of influence, corruption, human rights abuses, terrorism, and assassinations carried out by the security services or political elites of the Russian Federation or their proxies.

(2) Such other duties as the President may designate for purposes of this section.

(f) Staff.—The committee established by subsection (b) may employ such staff as the members of such committee consider appropriate.

(g) Budget Request.—A request for funds required for the functioning of the committee established by subsection (b) may be included in each budget for a fiscal year submitted by the President pursuant to section 1105(a) of title 31, United States Code.

(h) Annual Report.—

(1) Requirement.—Not later than 180 days after the date of the enactment of this Act, and annually thereafter, and consistent with the protection of intelligence

sources and methods, the committee established by subsection (b) shall submit to the appropriate committees of Congress a report describing steps being taken by the committee to counter active measures by Russia to exert covert influence.

(2) Matters Included.—Each report under paragraph (1) shall include a summary of the following:

(A) Active measures by Russia to exert covert influence during the previous year, including significant incidents and notable trends.

(B) Key initiatives of the committee.

(C) Implementation of the committee's initiatives by the heads of the agencies and departments of the United States Government specified in subsection (c)(1)(B).

(D) Analysis of the success of such initiatives.

(E) Changes to such initiatives from the previous year.

(3) Separate Reporting Requirement.—The requirement to submit an annual report under paragraph (1) is in addition to any other reporting requirements with respect to Russia.

1. The bill presented to Congress in December 2016 suggested that "media manipulation" by the Russian government was a problem to be eradicated. From what you've read so far, do you think this is something that should fall under the "media bias" heading, or do you think foreign interference is a different problem? Explain your reasoning.

2. The proposed bill is vague about what role Russia played in influencing the media and what should be done to stop it. Assuming Russia played a role in biasing the media toward a candidate during the 2016 election, what do you think could be done to stop this from happening again?

"STATEMENT BY PRESS SECRETARY SEAN SPICER," FROM THE WHITE HOUSE, JANUARY 21, 2017

MR. SPICER: Good evening. Thank you guys for coming. I know our first official press briefing is going to be on Monday, but I wanted to give you a few updates on the President's activities. But before I get to the news of the day, I think I'd like to discuss a little bit of the coverage of the last 24 hours.

Yesterday, at a time when our nation and the world was watching the peaceful transition of power and, as the President said, the transition and the balance of power from Washington to the citizens of the United States, some members of the media were engaged in deliberately false reporting. For all the talk about the proper use of Twitter, two instances yesterday stand out.

One was a particular egregious example in which a reporter falsely tweeted out that the bust of Martin Luther King, Jr. had been removed from the Oval Office. After it was pointed out that this was just plain wrong, the reporter casually reported and tweeted out and tried to claim that a Secret Service agent must have just been standing in front of it. This was irresponsible and reckless.

Secondly, photographs of the inaugural proceedings were intentionally framed in a way, in one particular tweet, to minimize the enormous support that had gathered on the National Mall. This was the first time in our nation's history that floor coverings have been used to protect the grass on the Mall. That had the effect of highlighting any areas where people were not standing, while in years past the grass eliminated this visual. This was also the first time that fencing and magnetometers went as far back on the Mall, preventing hundreds of thousands of people from being able to access the Mall as quickly as they had in inaugurations past.

Inaccurate numbers involving crowd size were also tweeted. No one had numbers, because the National Park

Service, which controls the National Mall, does not put any out. By the way, this applies to any attempts to try to count the number of protestors today in the same fashion.

We do know a few things, so let's go through the facts. We know that from the platform where the President was sworn in, to 4th Street, it holds about 250,000 people. From 4th Street to the media tent is about another 220,000. And from the media tent to the Washington Monument, another 250,000 people. All of this space was full when the President took the Oath of Office. We know that 420,000 people used the D.C. Metro public transit yesterday, which actually compares to 317,000 that used it for President Obama's last inaugural. This was the largest audience to ever witness an inauguration -- period -- both in person and around the globe. Even the New York Times printed a photograph showing a misrepresentation of the crowd in the original Tweet in their paper, which showed the full extent of the support, depth in crowd, and intensity that existed.

These attempts to lessen the enthusiasm of the inauguration are shameful and wrong. The President was also at the -- as you know, the President was also at the Central Intelligence Agency and greeted by a raucous overflow crowd of some 400-plus CIA employees. There were over 1,000 requests to attend, prompting the President to note that he'll have to come back to greet the rest. The employees were ecstatic that he's the new Commander-in-Chief, and he delivered them a powerful and important message. He told them he has their back, and they were grateful for that. They gave him a five-minute standing ovation at the end in a display of their patriotism and their enthusiasm for his presidency.

I'd also note that it's a shame that the CIA didn't have a CIA Director to be with him today when he visited, because the Democrats have chosen -- Senate Democrats are stalling the nomination of Mike Pompeo and playing politics with national security. That's what you guys should be writing and covering, instead of sowing division about tweets and false narratives.

The President is committed to unifying our country, and that was the focus of his inaugural address. This kind of dishonesty in the media, the challenging -- that bringing about our nation together is making it more difficult.

There's been a lot of talk in the media about the responsibility to hold Donald Trump accountable. And I'm here to tell you that it goes two ways. We're going to hold the press accountable, as well. The American people deserve better. And as long as he serves as the messenger for this incredible movement, he will take his message directly to the American people where his focus will always be.

And with that, a few other updates from the day. The President had a constructive conversation with Prime Minister Trudeau of Canada about strengthening the relationship between our two nations. They also discussed setting up additional meetings in the days to come, which we will follow up on. He also spoke to Prime Minister Peña Nieto of Mexico, and talked about a visit on trade, immigration and security that will occur on the 31st. The President will welcome his first foreign leader this Thursday when the United Kingdom's Theresa May will come to Washington -- on Friday.

Tomorrow, the President will oversee his Assistants to the President being sworn in. The staff will then have an ethics briefing, a briefing on the proper use and handling of classified information. Further updates as far as what he will do -- oh, and then in the evening, he will have a reception for law enforcement and first responders that helped support the inauguration.

Thank you guys for being here tonight. I will see you on Monday.

1. The press secretary says that while the media wants to hold the government accountable, the Trump administration will hold the media accountable. What do you think of this statement? Do you think these relationships are comparable? Why or why not?

2. Spicer suggests that by challenging the president, the media is making it harder for the new administration to unify the country and that media bias is partly to blame for the divide in the US. Do you think it's the media's job to challenge those in power or simply to report the facts? Is there a difference between these two tasks?

"REMARKS BY PRESIDENT TRUMP IN AFRICAN AMERICAN HISTORY MONTH LISTENING SESSION," FROM THE WHITE HOUSE, FEBRUARY 1, 2017

MR. WILLIAMS: Mr. President, I'm a member of what we call the media, but we try to be fair and objective. (Laughter.) Not all media seems to be the opposition party. There are those that see the good that you're doing. We report it. I'm just honored to have a seat at the table today.

THE PRESIDENT: Thank you. And it is -- I mean, a lot of the media is actually the opposition party. They're so biased and really is a disgrace. Some of you are fantastic and fair, but so much of the media is opposition party and knowingly saying incorrect things. So it's a very sad situation. But we seem to be doing well. It's almost like, in the meantime, we won. So maybe they don't have the influence they think, but they really are -- they really have to straighten out their act. They're very dishonest people.

1. President Trump refers to the media as "the opposition party." What do you think this sort of hostility between the press and the president will do to media bias?

2. The president refers to the media as a collective, singular entity. As you read in chapter one, this can be problematic. How could the Trump administration have better addressed the problem they saw without alienating friendly media outlets?

"CRIMINALIZING FORGERY OF FEDERAL DOCUMENTS," BY SENATOR JAMES M. INHOFE, FROM THE US SENATE, SEPTEMBER 28, 2004

Mr. President, the recent CBS incident involving the record of President Bush's service in the Texas Air National Guard sheds light on the need for a federal statute generally criminalizing the forgery of federal government documents. I believe that when it comes to crimes involving the fabrication of federal documents or writings, the federal government has an obligation to step in and show the offenders there are serious consequences.

Many experts initially doubted the authenticity of the memos in question, which negatively and falsely characterized President Bush's time in the Texas Air National Guard. We now believe these memos were created on a modern word-processing computer, rather the 1970s era typewriter as alleged in the original CBS story.

COLONEL KILLIAN & MARION KNOX

Lieutenant Colonel Jerry Killian was George Bush's commanding officer during his service in the Air National Guard in the 1970s. Unfortunately, Lt. Col. Killian passed away in 1984 and therefore could not defend his records.

However, Colonel Killian's secretary, Marion Knox, typed all of his correspondence between 1956 and 1979. Referring to the memos in question she said, "I know I didn't type 'em." It is clear that the documents CBS shared with American voters were more than suspect. After the fact—since CBS could not verify its reporting—I am pleased to see that CBS has belatedly retracted its story.

ADVANCE NOTICE TO KERRY CAMPAIGN

We also now know that the Kerry campaign was aware that CBS was planning to air the story four or five days before the fact, while the White House only received word on the eve of the story being broadcast.

This advance notice to the Kerry campaign is clear evidence of liberal bias. This bias highlights the intent of the liberal media to influence the American voters—rather than reporting objective news.

President Bush stands by his honorable service in the Air National Guard. He should not have had to worry about the threat of nefarious and petty efforts to defame his character.

CBS ACTIONS

I appreciated Dan Rather's words, "I want to say, personally and directly, I'm sorry." But saying I'm sorry just doesn't cut it.

Under much pressure, CBS has appointed an independent panel to investigate its reporting of the President's service in the Texas Air National Guard. I understand this panel is to be headed by former Attorney General Dick Thornburg and former Associated Press chief executive and former Pennsylvania Governor Lou Boccardi.

I agree with many of my colleagues from the House of Representatives who were dismayed that CBS, a network that should be responsible to report objective news, involved itself in a campaign that mislead the public and slandered the President. Therefore, I am proposing legislation to criminalize this type of action in general.

GENESIS OF THE LEGISLATION

After learning of the CBS scandal, I was curious about the penalty for the forgery of federal documents. In seeking the answer to this question, I called the Department of Justice. Their Congressional Relations Office promptly responded, "It depends."

The Justice Department stated that similar cases were often charged under the general sections of the Fraud and False Statements Chapter of the United States Criminal Code. These sections have proven quite useful to the prosecutors at the Department of Justice.

I learned of a loophole in the existing law regarding forgery and false statements. I learned that there are no general sections of the United States Criminal Code for Forgery and Counterfeiting. Officials from the Department of Justice noted the absence of a general standalone statute that criminalizes the actions of those who would forge documents of the federal government, regardless of the end they seek to achieve or what the documents are. Currently, the prosecution of such actions depends completely on the context and how forged documents were the means to an end.

Chapter 25 of Title 18 of the United States Code addresses various offenses in Counterfeiting and Forgery. The current 45 sections of the Counterfeiting and Forgery chapter essentially fall into four broad categories:

1. Financial obligations (including notes, postage, checks, securities, bonds, coins, money orders, debentures, et cetera),

2. Military and naval discharge certificates or official passes,

3. Transportation matters and motor vehicle documents, and

4. The seals of agencies (including courts, departments, and other agencies).

PIECEMEAL ENACTMENT OF COUNTERFEITING AND FORGERY CODE

The legislative history of the forty-five sections of the Counterfeiting and Forgery Chapter indicates that the sections were enacted piecemeal without a unifying, overarching section. If forgery takes place but does not fall into one of these sections, there is no penalty.

CONTRAST WITH FRAUD AND FALSE STATEMENTS CODE

Chapter 47 of Title 18 of the United States Code regarding Fraud and False Statements also contains disparate sections enacted piecemeal.

In contrast, however, the Fraud and False Statements Chapter does have an overarching section, Section 1001 that unifies its disparate, piecemeal parts.

In light of the recent situation involving President Bush's record, these broad, disparate sections need to include in general the fabrication of federal writings or memos.

EXAMINING THE APPLICABILITY OF OTHER STATUTES

In speaking with officials from the Department of Justice, I have also become aware of concerns over whether the existing statute regarding fraud, 18 § USCS § 1001, can be used in this CBS incident. Chapter 47 on Fraud and False Statements specifically condemns false statements, but only those with the intent of defrauding the federal government.

There are questions whether the "intent to defraud the United States or any agency thereof" is applicable or whether it could successfully be argued that instead it was the voters of the United States who were intentionally defrauded, distinguishing in certain fashion "United States" from "voters" or the like.

These concerns validate the need to criminalize the specific act of forging federal documents. Technically, in the CBS instance, it could be argued that the forged federal document did not monetarily or otherwise tangibly take away from the federal government. I would argue that it did harm the federal government by infringing on the federal government's copyright on its work. It certainly did affect millions of Americans by giving them a false and misleading impression about a presidential candidate. But it needs to be clarified.

NEED TO PROTECT FEDERAL SERVANTS GOVERNMENT-WIDE

As placed under Chapter 25 of Title 18, my bill would criminalize general forgery of federal government documents, including those that characterize or purport to characterize official federal activity, service, contract, obligation, duty, or property.

If someone attempts to forge, in the name of an official of the federal government, a document or memo that addresses an official government duty or act, that person should be held accountable. There needs to be a federal law prohibiting such forgery generally so that prosecution of the same does not fall through the cracks.

Currently, there is no catch-all section to address all forged federal writings, such as a note from one official to another about federal service.

I serve on the Senate Armed Services Committee and I honor those who serve in the National Guard. Not only has the CBS incident resulted in slander to the honorable National Guard service of President Bush, it also highlights the risk to the records of other military service members and, moreover, ALL federal servants government-wide.

A civil servant at the General Services Administration, which the Environment and Public Works Committee I chair happens to oversee, is equally deserving of being protected from a forgery of his or her work records. Right now there is no section in the forgery chapter of the US Code that specifically addresses protection for General Services Administration personnel. This omission is a problem we must correct.

PUBLISHING FORGED DOCUMENTS

My legislation also includes language to condemn those who, knowingly or negligently failing to know, transmit or present any such forged federal writing or record, which characterizes official federal activity or service. This general criminalization of publishing forged documents follows existing provisions of the forgery code. If a major news network broadcasts a story based on alleged federal documents, they must take the responsibility to verify those records.

WHO DID FORGE THE DOCUMENTS?

While CBS may not have taken part in the creation of the memos in question, and indeed I think I join the American people in yearning to know who did forge these memos, the network still touted them as verified and broadcast the forged memos as truthful to millions of American voters.

I look forward to a full criminal investigation of who did forge the documents.

INTENTIONAL OFFENSES VERSUS NEGLIGENT OFFENSES

I draw an analogy in distinguishing between murder and negligent homicide. Both are crimes. Murder is intentional and negligent homicide is not, but in both crimes someone was killed. While CBS may not have had the intention to deceive its audience, the false information was communicated when it was negligently not verified, and the damage was done nonetheless.

CONGRATULATING HARD WORK OF THOSE WHO DISCOVERED THE TRUTH

If it were not for the work of many astute people working through the Internet and otherwise, this travesty would not have been on its way to being exposed and fully prosecuted criminally. CBS and its surrogates pointedly disparaged the people who told the truth as mere second-class journalists of the Internet and cable television and talk-radio persuasions. Rather, it is CBS that has proven itself to be of even less than second-class journalism.

I note that numerous pundits have been discussing recently that the very vitality of the networks is faltering with the explosion of other media. Pundits have cited CBS's additional poor judgment in failing to cover the political conventions as well as other media outlets did. CBS owes a separate apology to those truth-tellers whom it slandered and who have shown better judgment than CBS.

MEDIA BIAS

I know that it can be difficult to communicate information without also conveying one's personal position on a matter. However, in a free society such as ours, the news media has a responsibility to work to be fair and balanced—to tell both sides of the story without letting journalistic spin cloud their judgment.

Television, print, and the Internet are powerful media. They shape our lives and provide some part of the education of our children, whether we like it or not. I believe the time has come for the media to take responsibility for its actions—rather than manipulate public opinion to lobby the causes and politicians the media support. Facts, not conclusions or erroneous records, should be reported. Elections are a powerful example of why journalists must hold themselves to the highest of standards. People can then synthesize information for themselves.

CONCLUSION

In conclusion, I argue that the media has a grave responsibility to ensure that what it reports is a true and accurate representation of the facts.

It could be argued that if CBS either forged the documents or knowingly represented forged document as being true, there is no penalty under the law.

We need to criminalize and establish the consequences for forging federal documents. I urge my colleagues to stand with me in supporting this appropriate and long-needed federal forgery legislation, and I ask unanimous consent that the text of the legislation and other accompanying documents be included in the record at this point.

1. The senator suggests that negligent reporting should be a punishable offense. Do you think journalistic negligence is a cause of media bias or an effect? Explain.

2. While the senator is speaking about a specific case of a media outlet using forged documents to verify a story, he says that the media has a responsibility to the people to be fair and present the facts accurately. Do you think investigative stories, such as the one CBS got in trouble for running with, can be presented without bias? Or does the nature of investigative reporting make it difficult to present a story objectively?

"PRIORITIES FOR HOMELAND SECURITY," STEVEN N. SIMON, FROM THE SENATE COMMITTEE ON HOMELAND SECURITY AND GOVERNMENTAL AFFAIRS, SEPTEMBER 12, 2006

Thank you for the opportunity to address the committee on this vital topic.

Just as a preamble, my remarks do not reflect the views of the Council on Foreign Relations, which does not have a corporate position on these matters.

My understanding of the Committee's objectives in holding this hearing is that witnesses should focus on the future and address themselves to issues that might help both Congress and the Executive branch set homeland security priorities. The Committee it seems to me is doing the right thing. Our vulnerability at home to terrorist assault, as well as to natural disasters, is essentially infinite. The fact is that not everything can be protected. Judicious decisions about what to protect given our wholesale and inevitable exposure to attack by clever and disciplined terrorists are essential.

What follows are my personal reflections on this vexing problem. Given the myriad threats to our infrastructure—critical and otherwise—and to the lives of our fellow citizens, other analysts will legitimately come to different conclusions about the best way to focus our collective efforts and especially those of the agencies under the jurisdiction of this committee, and of departments and agencies with which DHS must interact continuously and cooperatively in order to fulfill its daunting mandate.

I will concentrate on three issues: first, the importance of cities as terrorist havens and terrorist targets; second, the continuing significance to many jihadists of weapons of mass destruction (WMD); and third, the need to preserve the good will and sense of belonging of America's Muslim communities as a matter of national security, beyond the intrinsic virtues of a cohesive, considerate society in which citizens of all creeds can feel at home.

URBAN WARFARE

The jihad that has evolved since September 11th has become a war of cities. The transition from caves to condos, as one observer described this evolution, is impressive. Although the relatively remote, rural bases that incubated the jihad had strong advantages, especially given the centrality of social networks to the early jihad, municipalities have their own attractions. They offer anonymity, but also community, both of which can confer a kind of cover. Urban neighborhoods, with their numberless apartments, coffee-houses, mosques and Islamic centers, provide the setting for recruitment, clandestine meetings, preparation of weapons and other activities that form the terrorist enterprise. Moreover, the majority of urban areas in which jihadists have established a presence are not targets for air strikes, Hellfire missiles, or submarine-launched cruise missiles. Think of Muhammad Atta's Hamburg, or the Leeds of Muhammad Siddique Khan, orchestrator of the 7/7 bombings of the London underground and bus systems. Post-bin Laden jihadists are not the first militants to avail themselves of these tactical conveniences. The radical campaign in Egypt that began in mid-1970s was spawned in Cairo, one of the world's largest cities. And of course non-Muslim terrorist organizations, such as the Provisional Irish Republican Army (IRA), have long thrived in urban areas. It could be said that having adapted to city life, the jihad has really come into its own.

Qualities that favor the jihadists' defensive requirements do not tell the whole story. The other side is that cities are where their targets—both symbolic and of flesh-and-blood—are to be found in abundance and proximity. There are many aspects of Islamist militancy that are quintessentially modern. The transformation of cities into fields of jihad is a classic example of the movement's modernity. It is part and parcel of the post- World War II process of urbanization that swept the Middle East, North Africa and Pakistan. Large-scale migration of Muslims to Europe represents perhaps the last phase of this urbanizing process. In these cities, Muslims radicalized by a potent combination of powerful imagery in the media, socio-economic exclusion, and a set of simple, but internally consistent religious and ideological concepts, have ample targets for their hunger for retribution and duty—from their perspective—of self-defense. One of the striking features of contemporary Muslim public opinion to emerge from recent Pew polls is the degree to which Muslims in far-flung, diverse places have come to see themselves as having "more in common nowadays." This attitude can be seen at work in the United Kingdom, Spain, Germany, The Netherlands and Denmark. Events far removed geographically from these countries, especially developments in Iraq, have mobilized youth in each of their capitals.

New York has already shown itself to be a crucial target for jihadists. This great city was construed by al-Qaeda to be the beating heart of America's economy, which bin Laden believed he could cripple; the symbol of American arrogance as embodied by the "looming towers" of the World Trade Center; and the seat of Jewish power, which jihadists believe accounts for the global subordination of Muslim interests to America and

Israel. It is also a teeming city, whose large and densely packed population promised the most efficient path to a successful mass attack that—from a jihadist viewpoint— might begin to even the score with the United States. There is no reason to think that this conviction has weakened. Furthermore, New York City proffers the same advantages to the attacker as do all large cities.

The array of targeting opportunities in New York is wide. Although we can be perversely certain that the attack, when it comes, will be the one we least expected, some preliminary judgments are possible. Mass transportation, which the jihadists have attacked elsewhere with some success, the financial district or banks, symbols of authority, and perhaps schools, given al Qaeda's insistence on the need to avenge the tens of thousands of Muslim children it believes were deliberately killed by the U.S., either directly or through Israeli action thought to be sponsored by Washington. Car or truck bombs—the icon of urban violence in Iraq and used effectively before then in Lebanon and Argentina by Hezbollah and elsewhere by others including the IRA, the Basque separatist group ETA and the Baader-Meinhof gang—should also be expected at some point. Similarly, we might expect Palestinian style backpack bombs carried into restaurants or other public places by solitary suicidal attackers.

The implications of this analysis are, first, that community policing and extensive video surveillance probably need to be stepped up. In this kind of urban warfare, intelligence is acquired best by those who are most familiar with the terrain: police officers walking their beat. On the front line, they get to know their neighborhoods, the residents and the shopkeepers, form and cultivate relationships with local citizens, and develop a sense of the natural order of things and therefore of signs that something is out of the ordinary or warrants investigation. The pivotal role of local law enforcement is reinforced by the incapacity of federal authorities to gather information skillfully, discretely, effectively, and without alienating potential sources of intelligence. The FBI, in particular, presently lacks the numbers, skills, knowledge base and orientation to contribute.

This does not mean however that local law enforcement can or should operate in a vacuum, especially in light of connections that have been disclosed between the self-starter groups in the U.K. and al-Qaeda figures in Pakistan. On the contrary, local police need an umbilical connection to national intelligence agencies in order to connect the dots they're collecting on the ground. It is worth noting that the success of the UK counterterrorism effort in Northern Ireland was largely due the tight linkages between the local police, national police, and Britain's domestic intelligence agency that were forged early in the conflict.

Yet information sharing, which all parties claim to be essential, has not advanced significantly. In part this seems to be due to a lack of leadership, and in part to a slow pace of work that seems incommensurate with the urgency of the threat. Thus, issuance of U.S. government sponsored clearances for local police officers, the necessary first step toward sharing intelligence information, has lagged. Even the New York Police Department (NYPD), which has built a very aggressive intelligence collection program and uncommonly close ties to Washington intelligence agencies, has only about 350 cleared officers, or less than one per cent of the force. Many of these patrolmen and detectives have clearances via their status as military reservists rather than as police officers. Countrywide, cleared personnel are usually the handful of detailees to the local Joint Terrorism Task Force. The circle clearly needs to widen.

The other dimension to this issue is the apparent substitution of quantity for quality as Washington's criterion for information sharing with local law enforcement. This puts municipal authorities in the worst of both worlds. The information does not help them do their jobs better, while the sheer volume of unhelpful information can make it harder to manage their responsibilities.

The bigger question, however, is where these police officers will come from, at a time when State, local and federal budgets are under severe pressure. In the upcoming federal budget cycle the COPS program is again under pressure to be cut. This program has put more than 100,000 new police officers on the street over the last decade. Instead of eliminating this program it should be revamped to create the local intelligence capacity cities need.

WMD

Amid growing concerns about the vulnerability of ground transportation, civil aviation, financial institutions and landmarks to large bombs, one should not lose sight of the chemical, biological, radiological and nuclear threats. As many experts have usefully pointed out, jihadists, like other terrorists, prefer tried-and-true methods and shy away from technical innovation. This is certainly true as a general proposition, despite important exceptions, from the first use of dynamite by anarchists early in the 20th century to the experimentation with stabilized liquid explosives by Ramzi Ahmed Yousef in 1995.

Yet intramural jihadist tactical and strategic discussions frequently refer to the use of one or another form of weapon of mass destruction. Not every contributor to this debate defines the utility of these weapons in the same way. For some jihadists, WMDs are the golden key to a reversal of fortune, for which the Muslim world allegedly yearns. Others see these weapons in less apocalyptic terms and more as tools for "worldly war." For these jihadists, unconventional weapons are the indispensable instruments of the weaker party in an asymmetric struggle. Whether such a weapon is used in the belief that it will decisively settle the argument between Muslims and their chief enemy, or in pursuit of tactical effects meant to deter the enemy or deny him specific options, a toxic or radiological release or detonation of a nuclear weapon would have dramatic consequences.

The social and economic effects would obviously be proportional to the damage, but the baseline for these effects would be high. Thus, most experts believe that if such a weapon is used it is unlikely to cause mass casualties. Nevertheless, even an attack that took relatively few lives would have an emotional and psychological impact that could tear the fabric of our society and undermine the social contract between government and society. It would also have sizable, perhaps open-ended economic costs, especially if the attacks were repeated or authorities could not assure citizens that the attackers had all been captured or killed. The implication here is twofold. First, Washington must make consequence management a priority. This means not only allocating appropriated funds, but also establishing a high, federally defined performance standard that cities would have to meet reasonably swiftly. The reason for this emphasis on consequence management is simply that a well-planned attack will be difficult to prevent without an uncommon dose of good luck. This being the case, the surest way to stave off the worst emotional, political and economic damage is to show not only the victimized community, but also the American public that the effects of the attack are being handled with confidence and competence by local and federal authorities working quickly and smoothly—and in lockstep.

Efforts to do this have been broached repeatedly, ever since the second Nunn-Lugar bill was signed into law in 1996. Some of these initiatives failed because the government was not structured in a way that yielded a lead agency that could or would be held responsible for this important job. Now that we have a Department of Homeland Security, this impediment has been swept away. It is now time to systematize consequence management where it matters most, which is in large American cities.

The other implication is that Washington and local leaders must begin soon to educate the public about the kind of CBRN attacks that are likely to occur. The purpose is not to scare people. Rather, it is to ensure that Americans understand that for the foreseeable future, a CBRN attack will not necessarily equate to instant annihilation, that it is likely to kill or wound relatively small numbers, and that the federal government and local authorities are prepared for such an eventuality. This is easier said than done, owing to the non-trivial risk that terrorists acquire a weapon capable of a catastrophic nuclear yield. An educational initiative would have to acknowledge this possibility, even as it strove to counter the effect of the Katrina aftermath on public confidence in the competence of their government.

As part of this effort, dedicated broadcasting channels should be set up so that authorities can communicate with the public throughout a crisis and so that the public knows exactly how to "tune-in" to this source of information and guidance. Given the plethora of electronic media and the scarcity of bandwidth, operationalizing this recommendation will not be easy. In a crisis, however, we will wish we had it available.

It goes without saying that the trans-attack and post-attack message must be fully coordinated among federal state and local agencies. It will be just as vital for all these players to have decided beforehand who will be empowered to speak publicly and about what. In the absence of such discipline, the public will be awash in contradictory and inconsistent statements and quickly conclude that no one is in charge. This perception will fuel the panic and desperation latent in what will be a terrifying and unprecedented situation.

MUSLIM-AMERICANS

The 9/11 disaster showed that skilled, self-possessed and highly determined attackers could do tremendous damage to the homeland without having to rely on a support network within the United States. Halting and uneven progress on border security, especially at airports, has reduced the probability of this sort of attack by injecting uncertainty into terrorist calculations of their chances of getting in. Deterrence at that level does seem to work.

This type of attack, however, is not the adversary's sole option. Other approaches do require infrastructure, in the shape of cells that may or may not be linked to outside networks. A glance toward Western Europe, where this phenomenon seems to be well established, raises questions about circumstances here at home.

The conventional wisdom is that Europe's Muslim's discontent is a result of failed immigration policies that could not affect America's prosperous, happy Muslims, who have benefited from the welcoming embrace of our "melting pot" nation. This view may not reflect reality, even if it once did. Recent research shows that "the real story of American Muslims is one of accelerating alienation," which could produce a "rejectionist generation."

Muslims are increasingly choosing not to assimilate into American society, finding solace in their religious identity instead. Muslim students' associations on college campuses are growing rapidly as havens for Muslims who prefer not to socialize with non-Muslims, and Muslims are building Islamic schools as alternatives to a public school system perceived as inhospitable. To thwart media bias, Muslims are developing their own radio programs and publications. These initiatives may resemble those taken by other religious and ethnic groups in the United States since the nineteenth century to promote acceptance and assimilation. But the Muslims' situation differs in that many perceive their nation's foreign and domestic policy agenda as a campaign against their faith.

The domestic aftermath of the 9/11 attacks implied that a low religious profile was better for their health, that they couldn't take their civil rights for granted, and that their interests depended on the absence of serious future attacks within the United States. Iraq further dimmed America's promise to its Muslims. The U.S. Muslim community is deeply skeptical about U.S. democracy promotion, which many think are undercut by lack of due process at home and support for authoritarian rulers abroad. In particular, Muslims vocally decry what they see as the biased implementation of the USA PATRIOT Act and the absence of official American sympathy for the victimization of Muslims worldwide, especially Palestinians.

The evolving attitudes of non-Muslim Americans towards their Muslim compatriots are likely to spur alienation. According to a 2006 Gallup poll, a third of Americans admire "nothing" about the Muslim world. Nearly half of all Americans believe the U.S. government should restrict the civil liberties of Muslim Americans. Since September 11, they have faced increasing racism, employment and housing discrimination, and vandalism. The Justice Department has undertaken high-profile prosecutions based on meager evidence, flawed procedure or misidentification. Media coverage dwelling on the violence associated with radical Islam, and ignoring the respectable lifestyles of most American Muslims, along with rhetoric of some on the Christian Right casting the war on terrorism as a clash of religions, contributes to the public's misunderstanding of Islam.

To be sure, Muslims in the United States have shown no sign of violent protest, and American Muslims' relative prosperity may function as a brake on radicalization. Yet U.S. Muslims' post-9/11 insularity suggests that some, like many European Muslims, may seek psychological sanctuary in the umma—that is, the notional global community of Muslims. And the umma is where Osama bin Laden's brand of militancy has maximum traction.

The U.S. government also has not manifested trust in the nation's Muslims. While the pool of Muslims available for official duty may not be large, the federal government has made no serious efforts to recruit Muslims for confirmable policy positions. Meanwhile, mutual distrust has burgeoned. The U.S. administration should consult American Muslims directly and earnestly on foreign-policy issues, as it has customarily done with other politically important minority constituencies—e.g., American Jews with respect to Israel, Irish-Americans on Northern Ireland, and Greek-Americans as to Turkey and Cyprus. The difference here is that the electoral leverage of American Muslims is relatively weak. But their potential vulnerability to an incendiary ideology of confrontation that is being disseminated transnationally should override the normal course of domestic politics. Fear of being punished at the polls should not be the only incentive to be more attentive to Muslim concerns and anxieties.

Finally, the Madrid and London bombings only confirm that governments need to understand the campaign against transnational Islamist terrorism as an internal security problem to a much greater extent than they have so far. The current approach, however, has been simply to enforce a zero-tolerance immigration policy with respect to the Muslim community. This dispensation has the doubly perverse quality of being both ineffective in counter-terrorism terms and alienating with respect to Muslim Americans. Domestic law enforcement's ranks should also include more Muslims, both to improve the FBI's understanding of and links with Muslim communities and to give Muslims a sense of ownership of America's security challenges. American Muslims do not remotely pose the domestic threat that European Muslims do. To ensure it stays that way, they need to be embraced—not spurned.

I put this issue before the committee for lack of a better place. The challenge outlined here requires leadership and a program. Yet given the way our government is structured, there is no obvious lead agency, or special assistant to the President on the National Security Council or Homeland Security Council, to formulate a program or provide the leadership. We are not the first to face this conundrum. Several years ago, in the wake of a Whitehall study showing upwards of 10,000 al Qaeda supporters in Great Britain, Her Majesty's government tasked the Security Service— MI5—both to dismantle jihadist networks and devise a plan to win the hearts and minds of Britain's Muslim minority. Ultimately, the Security Services balked at a difficult job for which they had no experience or clear jurisdiction. We need to do better. Fortunately, unlike our sister democracies across the Atlantic, we have time. We must not squander it.

1. Simon says that in the years after 9/11, Muslims began creating their own media outlets to combat negative, anti-Muslim bias in the mainstream media. Do you think this sort of media creation combats media bias? Or do you think it creates an opposing bias?

2. In his statement, Simon claims the media focus only on the negative impact of radical Islam and not on the positive impact on society by average, respectable Muslims. Does this automatically point to media bias, or could other things be keeping the media from reporting on these more positive stories? Explain.

CHAPTER 3

WHAT THE COURTS SAY

The courts have been dealing with the media for decades, primarily in regards to the freedom of the press and of free speech as guaranteed by the First Amendment. But media bias isn't merely a matter of free speech, and the issues that have arisen have been far more complex than merely preventing government oversight of the news. In this chapter, you'll first read about how courts in Argentina, where free speech is not a guarantee, handle perceived media bias and what is expected of the relationship between the media and the government. Then you'll look at cases from the United States to explore what power the courts have over media coverage. In some of these cases, efforts to prevent media bias in the past have been revoked because it was feared they caused more bias than they prevented.

"SUPREME COURT TELLS ARGENTINA TO AVOID BIAS IN ALLOCATING ADS," FROM THE COMMITTEE TO PROTECT JOURNALISTS, MARCH 4, 2011

The Committee to Protect Journalists hails a ruling by Argentina's Supreme Court that calls for the omission of discriminatory criteria and "reasonable balance" in the allocation of state advertising. The ruling stems from a 2006 injunction filed by Editorial Perfil, the country's largest magazine publisher, claiming arbitrary distribution of official advertising.

"The Supreme Court ruling is a strong statement in support of press freedom in Argentina," said Carlos Lauría, CPJ's senior program coordinator for the Americas. "We call on Congress to take the next step and promote legislation that would limit the government's discretionary authority in allocating state advertising."

Argentina's highest court said Wednesday: "All media should receive official advertising: That is the difference between equal treatment and discriminatory treatment," according to local press reports. The court's unanimous decision upholds a 2009 ruling by a federal appeals court that withholding official advertising from several publications of Editorial Perfil violated freedom of the press as guaranteed in the Argentine constitution, CPJ research shows.

Perfil had filed a court injunction against the executive branch in July 2006, alleging that it was discriminated against by the Argentine government for its critical reporting. The company said its publications were denied government advertising and their journalists were barred access to official sources and events. The federal appeals court gave the government 15 days to place state ads in the company's weeklies *Noticias* and *Fortuna*, and its weekend paper *Perfil*. The government later appealed the decision before the Supreme Court, CPJ research shows.

Wednesday's decision builds on a 2007 Supreme Court ruling condemning the province of Neuquén for the withdrawal of state advertising from the national daily *Río Negro*. In the *Río Negro* case, the court stated that the government cannot curb the placement of official ads to the press arbitrarily.

CPJ and other analysts have found that the administration of President Cristina Kirchner, continuing a system institutionalized during the presidency of her husband, Néstor Kirchner, has manipulated the distribution of official advertizing to economically sanction critical media and reward those that support the government. Press freedom advocates have argued that the misappropriation of government advertising violates Articles 14 and 32 of the Argentine constitution, which prohibits censorship and guaranties freedom of the press, respectively, and Article 13 of the American Convention on Human Rights.

1. The Argentina Supreme Court ruled that the government cannot discriminate against media outlets when placing official advertisements in order to punish

outlets that have been critical of the government. Commercial advertisers would not be able to be held to this same standard. Do you think the Supreme Court of Argentina was right in ruling as it did? What effect do you think this ruling will have on people's belief that certain media outlets are biased against the Argentine government?

2. Do you think the same ruling would be made in the US Supreme Court if a similar problem arose in America? Why or why not?

NEW WORLD COMMUNICATIONS OF TAMPA, INC., D/B/A WTVT-TV, APPELLANT, V. JANE AKRE, APPELLEE, FROM THE DISTRICT COURT OF APPEAL OF FLORIDA, SECOND DISTRICT, FEBRUARY 14, 2003

KELLY, Judge.

New World Communications of Tampa, Inc., d/b/a WTVT-TV, a subsidiary of Fox Television, challenges a judgment entered against it for violating Florida's private sector whistle-blower's statute, section 448.102, Florida Statutes (Supp.1998). We reverse.

In December 1996, WTVT hired the appellee, Jane Akre, and her husband, Steve Wilson, as a husband-

and-wife investigative reporting team. Shortly after Akre and Wilson arrived at WTVT, they began working on a story about the use of synthetic bovine growth hormone ("BGH") in Florida dairy cattle. Their work on this story led to what could be characterized as an eight-month tug-of-war between the reporters and WTVT's management and lawyers over the content of the story. Each time the station asked Wilson and Akre to provide supporting documentation for statements in the story or to make changes in the content of the story, the reporters accused the station of attempting to distort the story to favor the manufacturer of BGH.

In September 1997, WTVT notified Akre and Wilson that it was exercising its option to terminate their employment contracts without cause. Akre and Wilson responded in writing to WTVT threatening to file a complaint with the Federal Communications Commission ("FCC") alleging that the station had "illegally" edited the still unfinished BGH report in violation of an FCC policy against federally licensed broadcasters deliberately distorting the news. The parties never resolved their differences regarding the content of the story, and consequently, the story never aired.

In April 1998, Akre and Wilson sued WTVT alleging, among other things, claims under the whistle-blower's statute. Those claims alleged that their terminations had been in retaliation for their resisting WTVT's attempts to distort or suppress the BGH story and for threatening to report the alleged news distortion to the FCC. Akre also brought claims for declaratory relief and for breach of contract. After a four-week trial, a jury found against Wilson on all of his claims. The trial court directed a verdict against Akre on her breach of contract claim, Akre abandoned her claim for declaratory relief, and the trial court let her whistle-blower claims go to the jury. The jury rejected all of Akre's claims except her claim that WTVT retaliated against her in response to her threat to disclose the alleged news distortion to the FCC. The jury awarded Akre $425,000 in damages.

While WTVT has raised a number of challenges to the judgment obtained by Akre, we need not address each challenge because we find as a threshold matter that Akre failed to state a claim under the whistle-blower's statute. The portion of the whistle-blower's statute pertinent to this appeal prohibits retaliation against employees who have "[d]isclosed, or threatened to disclose," employer conduct that "is in violation of" a law, rule, or regulation. § 448.102(1)(3). The statute defines a "law, rule or regula-tion" as "includ[ing] any statute or any rule or regulation adopted pursuant to any federal, state, or local statute or ordinance applicable to the employer and pertaining to the business." § 448.101(4), Fla. Stat. (1997). We agree with WTVT that the FCC's policy against the intentional falsification of the news-which the FCC has called its "news distortion policy"-does not qualify as the required "law, rule, or regulation" under section 448.102.

The FCC has never published its news distor-tion policy as a regulation with definitive elements and defenses. Instead, the FCC has developed the policy through the adjudicatory process in decisions resolving challenges to broadcasters' licenses. The policy's roots can be traced to 1949 when the FCC first expressed its concern regarding deceptive news in very general terms stating that "[a] licensee would be abusing his position as a public trustee of these important means of mass communications were he to withhold from expression over his facilities relevant news of facts concerning a controversy or to slant or distort the news." See Chad Raphael, The FCC's Broadcast News Distortion Rules: Regulation by Drooping Eyelid, 6 Comm. L. & Policy 485, 494 (2001) (quoting Editorializing by Broadcast Licensees, 13 F.C.C. 1246, 1246 (1949)).

The policy did not begin to take shape, however, until 1969 when the FCC was called upon to investigate complaints regarding news distortion. Raphael at 494. Notably, the FCC did not take the initiative to investigate these complaints, but rather acted only after Congress referred complaints it had received to the FCC. In a series of opinions issued in licensing proceedings between 1969 and 1973, the FCC stated that when considering the status of a broadcaster's license, it would take into consideration proven instances of "deliberate news distortion," also called "intentional falsification of the news" or "rigging or slanting the news." In re CBS Program "Hunger in America", 20 F.C.C.2d 143, 150-51 (1969). This series of FCC opinions has come to be known as the FCC's news distortion policy.

Akre argues that the FCC's policy is a rule as defined by section 120.52(15), Florida Statutes (1997), which provides:

> "Rule" means each agency statement of general applicability that implements, interprets, or prescribes law or policy or describes the procedure or practice requirements of an agency and includes any form which imposes any requirement or solicits any information not specifically required by statute or by an existing rule.

Even if we agreed with Akre that the FCC's news distortion policy was a "rule" as defined by section 120.52(15), her argument overlooks the fact that the whistle-blower's statute specifically limits the definition of "rule" to an "adopted" rule. § 448.101(4). "This limitation to 'adopted' material only appears deliberate, and well serves the public by hinging civil liability upon matters of which due notice, actual or imputed, has been conveyed." <u>Forrester v. John B. Phipps</u>, Inc., 643 So.2d 1109 (Fla. 1st DCA 1994). We find the legislature's use of the word "adopted" in the statute to be a limitation on the scope of conduct that will subject an employer to liability under the statute.

It is undisputed that the FCC's news distortion policy has never been "adopted" as defined by section 120.54, Florida Statutes (1997). In that regard, Akre notes that federal agencies may announce general policies and interpretive principles through the adjudicative process and argues that the fact that "the FCC adopted the news distortion policy through an adjudicative process does not affect its validity or enforceability as a matter of federal law." This argument is flawed in two respects. First, federal law recognizes a dichotomy between rulemaking and adjudication; it does not equate the two. <u>See Bowen v. Georgetown Univ. Hosp.</u>, 488 U.S. 204, 109 S.Ct. 468, 102 L.Ed.2d 493 (1988) (Scalia, J., concurring). Second, while federal agencies may have discretion to formulate policy through the adjudicative process, the same is not true under Florida law. The Florida Legislature has limited state agencies' discretion to formulate policy through the adjudicative process by requiring agencies to formally adopt each agency statement that fits the definition of a "rule" under section 120.52. <u>See</u> §120.54. As noted above, the legislature›s use of the word "adopted" in the whistle-blower›s statute was deliberate and was intended to limit the scope of conduct that will subject an employer to liability.

This limitation is consistent with the legislature's requirement that agency statements that fit the definition of a "rule" be formally adopted. Recognizing an uncodified agency policy developed through the adjudicative process as the equivalent of a formally adopted rule is not consistent with this policy, and it would expand the scope of conduct that could subject an employer to liability beyond what Florida's Legislature could have contemplated when it enacted the whistle-blower's statute.

Because the FCC's news distortion policy is not a "law, rule, or regulation" under section 448.102, Akre has failed to state a claim under the whistle-blower's statute. Accordingly, we reverse the judgment in her favor and remand for entry of a judgment in favor of WTVT.

Reversed and remanded.

CASANUEVA, J., and GREEN, OLIVER L.,
Senior Judge, Concur.

NEW WORLD COMMUNICATIONS OF TAMPA, INC., D/B/A WTVT-TV, APPELLANT, V. JANE AKRE, APPELLEE, FROM THE DISTRICT COURT OF APPEAL OF FLORIDA, SECOND DISTRICT, FEBRUARY 25, 2004

ORDER ON APPELLEE'S MOTION FOR REHEARING, MOTION FOR CLARIFICATION, MOTION FOR REHEARING EN BANC, AND MOTION FOR CERTIFICATION OF QUESTION OF GREAT PUBLIC IMPORTANCE.

KELLY, Judge.

This court entered an order granting appellate attorney's fees to the appellant, New World Communications of Tampa, Inc., d/b/a WTVT-TV, a subsidiary of Fox Television. Thereafter, the appellee, Jane Akre, sought rehearing, clarification, rehearing en banc, and certification of a question of great public importance. We grant Akre's requests for rehearing and clarification and deny her requests for rehearing en banc and certification.

WTVT appealed a final judgment entered against it for violating Florida's private sector whistle-blower's statute, section 448.102, Florida Statutes (1997). The final judgment was entered pursuant to a jury verdict awarding Akre $425,000 in damages. We reversed after concluding that Akre had failed to state a claim under the whistle-blower's statute. We also granted WTVT's motion for appellate attorney's fees under section 448.104, Florida Statutes (1997), which states, "[a] court may award reasonable attorney's fees, court costs, and expenses to the prevailing party."

In her motion for rehearing, Akre argues that because section 448.104 authorizes an award of attorney's fees to prevailing defendants as well as to prevailing plaintiffs, this court should apply the standard articulated in Christiansburg Garment Co. v. Equal Employment Opportunity Commission, 434 U.S. 412, 421, 98 S.Ct. 694, 54 L.Ed.2d 648 (1978). In Christiansburg, the Court had to determine the proper standard for an award of attorney's fees to a prevailing defendant in an action brought under Title VII of the Civil Rights Act of 1964. Title VII gives courts discretion to award fees to the prevailing party, as does section 448.104, but it does not give any indication of when a court should award fees to a prevailing plaintiff or a prevailing defendant.

The Christiansburg Court concluded that equitable considerations embodied in Title VII justified applying different standards depending on whether the prevailing party was a plaintiff or a defendant. The Court found that while fees should be awarded to every prevailing plaintiff unless special circumstances would make such an award unjust, fees should only be awarded to a prevailing defendant when the plaintiff's action was "frivolous, unreasonable, or without foundation." Christiansburg, 434 U.S. at 420.

We do not agree with Akre's contention that this same standard should apply to an action brought under Florida's whistle-blower's statute. We are not persuaded that the reasons cited by the <u>Christiansburg</u> Court for applying different standards to prevailing plaintiffs and defendants apply to cases brought under section 448.103. To the extent that this question has been addressed by other courts, they have likewise concluded that the <u>Christiansburg</u> standard is not applicable to fee awards under section 448.104. <u>See Gamb v. Hilton Hotels Corp.</u>, No. 95-466-CIV-ORL-19, 1997 WL 893874 (M.D.Fla. Sept.26, 1997), <u>aff'd</u>, 132 F.3d 46 (11th Cir.1997); <u>McGregor v. Bd. of County Comm'rs</u>, 130 F.R.D. 464 (S.D.Fla.1990), <u>aff'd</u>, 956 F.2d 1017 (11th Cir.1992).

Nevertheless, because section 448.104 is not mandatory, we must consider whether to exercise our discretion and make such an award in this case. Under the circumstances of this appeal, we conclude that WTVT is not entitled to appellate attorney's fees. Akre came to this court as an appellee defending a final judgment entered in her favor at the conclusion of a jury trial. We do not believe that it is either realistic or good policy to require an appellee who has obtained a favorable jury verdict to abandon it on appeal or risk an award of attorney's fees if it is reversed.

We reach this conclusion even though the whistle-blower aspect of Akre's case was without legal merit from its inception. This court has held that because all final judgments have a presumption of correctness, attempting to uphold one is not frivolous. <u>Cf. Dep't of Highway Safety & Motor Vehicles v. Salter</u>, 710 So.2d 1039 (Fla. 2d DCA 1998).[1] Accordingly, even the lack of legal merit in Akre's position does not convince us that we should exercise our discretion to award appellate attorney's fees to WTVT.

`We emphasize that we are only considering the issue of a proper exercise of discretion for an award of appellate attorney's fees. On remand, the trial court will have to make its own determination regarding whether to award trial court attorney's fees to WTVT as the prevailing party. To be entitled to such an award, however, WTVT does not have to demonstrate that Akre's suit was frivolous.

No further motions for rehearing will be entertained.

CASANUEVA, J., and GREEN, OLIVER L.,
Senior Judge, Concur.

1. A local news station was sued by a former reporter for attempting to force the reporter to change the scope of her reporting to better align with the views of the group being investigated. After reading the case, do you think WTVT was showing bias in their attempts to change the reporter's coverage?

2. If you were the reporter in this case, what would you have done?

RED LION BROADCASTING CO., INC. V. FCC, 395 U.S. 367 (1969), FROM THE UNITED STATES SUPREME COURT, JUNE 9, 1969

CERTIORARI TO THE UNITED STATES COURT OF APPEALS

FOR THE DISTRICT OF COLUMBIA CIRCUIT

SYLLABUS

The Federal Communications Commission (FCC) has for many years imposed on broadcasters a "fairness doctrine," requiring that public issues be presented by broadcasters and that each side of those issues be given fair coverage. In No. 2, the FCC declared that petitioner Red Lion Broadcasting Co. had failed to meet its obligation under the fairness doctrine when it carried a program which constituted a personal attack on one Cook, and ordered it to send a transcript of the broadcast to Cook and provide reply time, whether or not Cook would pay for it. The Court of Appeals upheld the FCC's position. After the commencement of the *Red Lion* litigation, the FCC began a rulemaking proceeding to make the personal attack aspect of the fairness doctrine more precise and more readily enforceable, and to specify its rules relating to political editorials. The rules, as adopted and amended, were held unconstitutional by the Court of Appeals in *RTNDA* (No. 717) as abridging the freedoms of speech and press.

Held:

1. The history of the fairness doctrine and of related legislation shows that the FCC's action in the *Red Lion* case did not exceed its authority, and that, in adopting the new regulations, the FCC was implementing congressional policy. Pp. 395 U. S. 375-386.

(a) The fairness doctrine began shortly after the Federal Radio Commission was established to allocate frequencies among competing applicants in the public interest, and insofar as there is an affirmative obligation of the broadcaster to see that both sides are presented, the personal attack doctrine and regulations do not differ from the fairness doctrine. Pp. 395 U. S. 375-379.

(b) The FCC's statutory mandate to see that broadcasters operate in the public interest and Congress' reaffirmation, in the 1959 amendment to § 315 of the Communications Act, of the FCC's view that the fairness doctrine inhered in the public interest standard, support the conclusion that the doctrine and its component personal attack and political editorializing' regulations are a legitimate exercise of congressionally delegated authority. Pp. 395 U. S. 379-386.

2. The fairness doctrine and its specific manifestations in the personal attack and political editorial rules do not violate the First Amendment. Pp. 395 U. S. 386-401.

(a) The First Amendment is relevant to public broadcasting, but it is the right of the viewing and listening public, and not the right of the broadcasters, which is paramount. Pp. 395 U. S. 386-390.

(b) The First Amendment does not protect private censorship by broadcasters who are licensed by the Government to use a scarce resource which is denied to others. Pp. 395 U. S. 390-392.

(c) The danger that licensees will eliminate coverage of controversial issues as a result of the personal attack and political editorial rules is, at best, speculative, and, in any event, the FCC has authority to guard against this danger. Pp. 395 U. S. 392-395.

(d) There was nothing vague about the FCC's specific ruling in the *Red Lion* case, and the regulations at issue in No. 717 could be employed in precisely the same way as the fairness doctrine in *Red Lion*. It is not necessary to decide every aspect of the fairness doctrine to decide these cases. Problems involving more extreme applications or more difficult constitutional questions will be dealt with if and when they arise. Pp. 395 U. S. 395-396.

(e) It has not been shown that the scarcity of broadcast frequencies, which impelled governmental regulation, is entirely a thing of the past, as new uses for the frequency spectrum have kept pace with improved technology and more efficient utilization of that spectrum. Pp. 395 U. S. 396-400.

No. 2, 127 U.S.App.D.C. 129, 381 F.2d 908, affirmed; No. 717, 400 F.2d 1002, reversed and remanded.

MR. JUSTICE WHITE delivered the opinion of the Court

The Federal Communications Commission has for many years imposed on radio and television broadcasters the requirement that discussion of public issues be presented on broadcast stations, and that each side of those issues must be given fair coverage. This is known as the fairness doctrine, which originated very early in the history of broadcasting and has maintained its present outlines for some time. It is an obligation whose content has been defined in a long series of FCC rulings in particular cases, and which is distinct from the statutory requirement of § 315 of the Communications Act[1] that equal time be allotted all qualified candidates for public office. Two aspects of the fairness doctrine, relating to personal attacks in the context of controversial public issues and to political editorializing, were codified more precisely in the form of FCC regulations in 1967. The two cases before us now, which were decided separately below, challenge the constitutional and statutory bases of the doctrine and component rules. *Red Lion* involves the application of the fairness doctrine to a particular broadcast, and RTNDA arises as an action to review the FCC's 1967 promulgation of the personal attack and political editorializing regulations, which were laid down after the Red Lion litigation had begun.

I

A

The Red Lion Broadcasting Company is licensed to operate a Pennsylvania radio station, WGCB. On November 27, 1964,

WGCB carried a 15-minute broadcast by the Reverend Billy James Hargis as part of a "Christian Crusade" series. A book by Fred J. Cook entitled "Goldwater -- Extremist on the Right" was discussed by Hargis, who said that Cook had been fired by a newspaper for making false charges against city officials; that Cook had then worked for a Communist-affiliated publication; that he had defended Alger Hiss and attacked J. Edgar Hoover and the Central Intelligence Agency, and that he had now written a "book to smear and destroy Barry Goldwater."[2] When Cook heard of the broadcast, he concluded that he had been personally attacked and demanded free reply time, which the station refused. After an exchange of letters among Cook, Red Lion, and the FCC, the FCC declared that the Hargis broadcast constituted a personal attack on Cook; that Red Lion had failed to meet its obligation under the fairness doctrine as expressed in *Times-Mirror Broadcasting Co.*, 24 P & F Radio Reg. 404 (1962), to send a tape, transcript, or summary of the broadcast to Cook and offer him reply time, and that the station must provide reply time whether or not Cook would pay for it. On review in the Court of Appeals for the District of Columbia Circuit,[3] the FCC's position was upheld as constitutional and otherwise proper. 127 U.S.App.D.C. 129, 381 F.2d 908 (1967).

B

Not long after the *Red Lion* litigation was begun, the FCC issued a Notice of Proposed Rule Making, 31 Fed.Reg. 5710, with an eye to making the personal attack aspect of the fairness doctrine more precise and more readily enforceable, and to specifying its rules relating to political editorials. After considering written comments supporting and opposing the rules, the FCC adopted them substantially as proposed, 32

Fed.Reg. 10303. Twice amended, 32 Fed.Reg. 11531, 33 Fed. Reg. 5362, the rules were held unconstitutional in the RTNDA litigation by the Court of Appeals for the Seventh Circuit, on review of the rulemaking proceeding, as abridging the freedoms of speech and press. 400 F.2d 1002 (1968).

As they now stand amended, the regulations read as follows:

"Personal attacks; political editorials."

"(a) When, during the presentation of views on a controversial issue of public importance, an attack is made upon the honesty, character, integrity or like personal qualities of an identified person or group, the licensee shall, within a reasonable time and in no event later than 1 week after the attack, transmit to the person or group attacked(1) notification of the date, time and identification of the broadcast; (2) a script or tape (or an accurate summary if a script or tape is not available) of the attack, and (3) an offer of a reasonable opportunity to respond over the licensee's facilities."

"(b) The provisions of paragraph (a) of this section shall not be applicable (1) to attacks on foreign groups or foreign public figures; (2) to personal attacks which are made by legally qualified candidates, their authorized spokesmen, or those associated with them in the campaign, on other such candidates, their authorized spokesmen, or persons associated with the candidates in the campaign, and (3) to bona fide newscasts, bona fide news interviews, and on-the-spot coverage of a bona fide news event (including commentary or analysis contained in the foregoing programs, but the provisions of paragraph (a) of this section shall be applicable to editorials of the licensee)."

"NOTE: The fairness doctrine is applicable to situations coming within [(3)], above, and, in a specific factual situation, may be applicable in the general area of political broadcasts [(2)], above. See section 315(a) of the Act, 47 U.S.C. 315(a); Public Notice: Applicability of the Fairness Doctrine in the Handling of Controversial Issues of Public Importance. 29 F. R. 10415. The categories listed in [(3)] are the same as those specified in section 315(a) of the Act."

"(c) Where a licensee, in an editorial, (i) endorses or (ii) opposes a legally qualified candidate or candidates, the licensee shall, within 24 hours after the editorial, transmit to respectively (i) the other qualified candidate or candidates for the same office or (ii) the candidate opposed in the editorial (1) notification of the date and the time of the editorial; (2) a script or tape of the editorial, and (3) an offer of a reasonable opportunity for a candidate or a spokesman of the candidate to respond over the licensee's facilities: Provided, however, That where such editorials are broadcast within 72 hours prior to the day of the election, the licensee shall comply with the provisions of this paragraph sufficiently far in advance of the broadcast to enable the candidate or candidates to have a reasonable opportunity to prepare a response and to present it in a timely fashion."

47 CFR §§ 73.123, 73.300, 73.598, 73.679 (all identical).

C

Believing that the specific application of the fairness doctrine in *Red Lion*, and the promulgation of the regulations
in *RTNDA*, are both authorized by Congress and enhance,
rather than abridge, the freedoms of speech and press
protected by the First Amendment, we hold them valid and
constitutional, reversing the judgment below in *RTNDA*
and affirming the judgment below in *Red Lion*.

II

The history of the emergence of the fairness doctrine and
of the related legislation shows that the Commission's
action in the *Red Lion* case did not exceed its authority,
and that, in adopting the new regulations, the Commission was implementing congressional policy, rather than
embarking on a frolic of its own.

A

Before 1927, the allocation of frequencies was left entirely
to the private sector, and the result was chaos.[4]
   It quickly became apparent that broadcast frequencies
constituted a scarce resource whose use could be regulated
and rationalized only by the Government. Without government control, the medium would be of little use because of
the cacaphony of competing voices, none of which could be
clearly and predictably heard.[5] Consequently, the Federal
Radio Commission was established to allocate frequencies
among competing applicants in a manner responsive to the
public "convenience, interest, or necessity."[6]
   Very shortly thereafter, the Commission expressed
its view that the

"public interest requires ample play for the free and fair competition of opposing views, and the commission believes that the principle applies . . . to all discussions of issues of importance to the public."

Great Lakes Broadcasting Co., 3 F.R.C.Ann.Rep. 32, 33 (1929), *rev'd on other grounds*, 59 App.D.C.197, 37 F.2d 993, *cert. dismissed*, 281 U.S. 706 (1930). This doctrine was applied through denial of license renewals or construction permits, both by the FRC, *Trinity Methodist Church, South v. FRC*, 61 App.D.C. 311, 62 F.2d 850 (1932), *cert. denied*, 288 U.S. 599 (1933), and its successor *FCC*, *Young People's Association for the Propagation of the Gospel*, 6 F.C.C. 178 (1938). After an extended period during which the licensee was obliged not only to cover and to cover fairly the views of others but also to refrain from expressing his own personal views, *Mayflower Broadcasting Corp.*, 8 F.C.C. 333 (1940), the latter limitation on the licensee was abandoned, and the doctrine developed into its present form.

There is a twofold duty laid down by the FCC's decisions and described by the 1949 Report on Editorializing by Broadcast Licensees, 13 F.C.C. 1246 (1949). The broadcaster must give adequate coverage to public issues, *United Broadcasting Co.*, 10 F.C.C. 515 (1945), and coverage must be fair in that it accurately reflects the opposing views. *New Broadcasting Co.*, 6 P & F Radio Reg. 258 (1950). This must be done at the broadcaster's own expense if sponsorship is unavailable. *Cullman Broadcasting Co.*, 25 P & F Radio Reg. 895 (1963).

Moreover, the duty must be met by programming obtained at the licensee's own initiative if available from no other source. *John J. Dempsey*, 6 P & F Radio Reg.

615 (1950); *see Metropolitan Broadcasting Corp.*, 19 P & F Radio Reg. 602 (1960); *The Evening News Assn.*, 6 P & F Radio Reg. 283 (1950). The Federal Radio Commission had imposed these two basic duties on broadcasters since the outset, *Great Lakes Broadcasting Co.*, 3 F.R.C.Ann.Rep. 32 (1929), *rev'd on other grounds*, 59 App.D.C.197, 37 F.2d 993, *cert. dismissed*, 281 U.S. 706 (1930); *Chicago Federation of Labor v. FRC*, 3 F.R.C.Ann.Rep. 36 (1029), *aff'd*, 59 App.D.C. 333, 41 F.2d 422 (1930); *KFKB Broadcasting Assn. v. FRC*, 60 App.D.C. 79, 47 F.2d 670 (1931), and in particular respects the personal attack rules and regulations at issue here have spelled them out in greater detail.

When a personal attack has been made on a figure involved in a public issue, both the doctrine of cases such as *Red Lion* and *Times-Mirror Broadcasting Co.*, 24 P & F Radio Reg. 404 (1962), and also the 1967 regulations at issue in RTNDA, require that the individual attacked himself be offered an opportunity to respond. Likewise, where one candidate is endorsed in a political editorial, the other candidates must themselves be offered reply time to use personally or through a spokesman. These obligations differ from the general fairness requirement that issues be presented, and presented with coverage of competing views, in that the broadcaster does not have the option of presenting the attacked party's side himself or choosing a third party to represent that side. But insofar as there is an obligation of the broadcaster to see that both sides are presented, and insofar as that is an affirmative obligation, the personal attack doctrine and regulations do not differ from the preceding fairness doctrine. The simple fact that the attacked men or unendorsed candidates may respond themselves or through agents is not a critical distinction, and, indeed, it is not unreasonable for the FCC to conclude that the objective of adequate presentation of all sides may best be served by allowing those most closely affected to make the response, rather than leaving the response in the hands of the station which has attacked their candidacies, endorsed their opponents, or carried a personal attack upon them.

B

The statutory authority of the FCC to promulgate these regulations derives from the mandate to the "Commission from time to time, as public convenience, interest, or necessity requires" to promulgate

> "such rules and regulations and prescribe such restrictions and conditions . . . as may be necessary to carry out the provisions of this chapter. . . ."

47 U.S.C. § 303 and § 303(r).[7] The Commission is specifically directed to consider the demands of the public interest in the course of granting licenses, 47 U.S.C. §§ 307(a), 309(a); renewing them, 47 U.S.C. § 307, and modifying them. *Ibid.* Moreover, the FCC has included among the conditions of the Red Lion license itself the requirement that operation of the station be carried out in the public interest, 47 U.S.C. § 309(h). This mandate to the FCC to assure that broadcasters operate in the public interest is a broad one, a power "not niggardly but expansive," *National Broadcasting Co. v. United States*, 319 U. S. 190, 319 U. S. 219 (1943), whose validity we have long upheld. *FCC v. Pottsville Broadcasting Co.*, 309 U. S. 134, 309 U. S. 138 (1940); *FCC v. RCA Communications, Inc.*, 346 U. S. 86, 346 U. S. 90 (1953); *FRC v. Nelson Bros. Bond & Mortgage Co.*, 289 U. S. 266, 289 U. S. 285 (1933). It is broad enough to encompass these regulations.

The fairness doctrine finds specific recognition in statutory form, is in part modeled on explicit statutory provisions relating to political candidates, and is approvingly reflected in legislative history.

In 1959, the Congress amended the statutory requirement of § 315 that equal time be accorded each political candidate to except certain appearances on news programs, but added that this constituted no exception

"from the obligation imposed upon them under this Act to operate in the public interest and to afford reasonable opportunity for the discussion of conflicting views on issues of public importance."

Act of September 14, 1959, § 1, 73 Stat. 557, amending 47 U.S.C. § 315(a) (emphasis added). This language makes it very plain that Congress, in 1959, announced that the phrase "public interest," which had been in the Act since 1927, imposed a duty on broadcasters to discuss both sides of controversial public issues. In other words, the amendment vindicated the FCC's general view that the fairness doctrine inhered in the public interest standard. Subsequent legislation declaring the intent of an earlier statute is entitled to great weight in statutory construction.[8] And here this principle is given special force by the equally venerable principle that the construction of a statute by those charged with its execution should be followed unless there are compelling indications that it is wrong,[9] especially when Congress has refused to alter the administrative construction.[10] Here, the Congress has not just kept its silence by refusing to overturn the administrative construction,[11] but has ratified it with positive legislation. Thirty years of consistent administrative construction left undisturbed by Congress until 1959, when that construction was expressly accepted, reinforce the natural conclusion that the public interest language of the Act authorized the Commission to require licensees to use their stations for discussion of public issues, and that the FCC is free to implement this requirement by reasonable rules and regulations which fall short of abridgment of the freedom of speech and press, and of the censorship proscribed by § 326 of the Act.[12]

The objectives of § 315 themselves could readily be circumvented but for the complementary fairness doctrine ratified by § 315. The section applies only to campaign appearances by candidates, and not by family, friends, campaign managers, or other supporters. Without the fairness doctrine, then, a licensee could ban all campaign appearances by candidates themselves from the air[13] and proceed to deliver over his station entirely to the supporters of one slate of candidates, to the exclusion of all others. In this way, the broadcaster could have a far greater impact on the favored candidacy than he could by simply allowing a spot appearance by the candidate himself. It is the fairness doctrine as an aspect of the obligation to operate in the public interest, rather than § 315, which prohibits the broadcaster from taking such a step.

The legislative history reinforces this view of the effect of the 1959 amendment. Even before the language relevant here was added, the Senate report on amending § 315 noted that

"broadcast frequencies are limited, and, therefore, they have been necessarily considered a public trust. Every licensee who is fortunate in obtaining a license is mandated to operate in the public interest, and has assumed the obligation of presenting important public questions fairly and without bias."

S.Rep. No. 562, 86th Cong., 1st Sess., 8-9 (1959). See also, specifically adverting to Federal Communications Commission doctrine, *id.* at 13.

Rather than leave this approval solely in the legislative history, Senator Proxmire suggested an amendment to make it part of the Act. 105 Cong. Rec. 14457. This amendment, which Senator Pastore, a manager of the bill and a ranking member of the Senate Committee, considered "rather surplusage," 105 Cong.Rec. 14462, constituted a positive statement of doctrine,[14] and was altered to the present merely approving language in the conference committee. In explaining the language to the Senate after the committee changes, Senator Pastore said:

"We insisted that that provision remain in the bill, to be a continuing reminder and admonition to the Federal Communications Commission and to the broadcasters alike that we were not abandoning the philosophy that gave birth to section 316, in giving the people the right to have a full and complete disclosure of conflicting views on news of interest to the people of the country."

105 Cong.Rec. 17830. Senator Scott, another Senate manager, added that: "It is intended to encompass all legitimate areas of public importance which are controversial," not just politics. 105 Cong.Rec. 17831.

It is true that the personal attack aspect of the fairness doctrine was not actually adjudicated until after 1959, so that Congress then did not have those rules specifically before it. However, the obligation to offer time to reply to a personal attack was presaged by the FCC's 1949 Report on Editorializing, which the FCC views as the principal summary of its *ratio decidendi* in cases in this area:

> "In determining whether to honor specific requests for time, the station will inevitably be confronted with such questions as . . . whether there may not be other available groups or individuals who might be more appropriate spokesmen for the particular point of view than the person making the request. The latter's personal involvement in the controversy may also be a factor which must be considered, for elementary considerations of fairness may dictate that time be allocated to a person or group which has been specifically attacked over the station, where otherwise no such obligation would exist."

13 F.C.C. at 1251-1252.

When the Congress ratified the FCC's implication of a fairness doctrine in 1959, it did not, of course, approve every past decision or pronouncement by the Commission on this subject, or give it a completely free hand for the future. The statutory authority does not go so far. But we cannot say that, when a station publishes personal attacks or endorses political candidates, it is a misconstruction of the public interest standard to require the station to offer time for a response, rather than to leave the response entirely within the control of the station which has attacked either the candidacies or the men who wish to reply in their own defense. When a broadcaster grants time to a political candidate, Congress itself requires that equal time be offered to his opponents. It would exceed our competence to hold that the Commission is unauthorized by the statute to employ a similar device where personal attacks or political editorials are broadcast by a radio or television station.

In light of the fact that the "public interest" in broadcasting clearly encompasses the presentation of vigorous debate of controversial issues of importance and concern to the public, the fact that the FCC has rested upon that language from its very inception a doctrine that these issues must be discussed, and fairly, and the fact that Congress has acknowledged that the analogous provisions of § 315 are not preclusive in this area, and knowingly preserved the FCC's complementary efforts, we think the fairness doctrine and its component personal attack and political editorializing regulations are a legitimate exercise of congressionally delegated authority. The Communications Act is not notable for the precision of its substantive standards, and, in this respect the explicit provisions of § 315, and the doctrine and rules at issue here which are closely modeled upon that section, are far more explicit than the generalized "public interest" standard in which the Commission ordinarily finds its sole guidance, and which we have held a broad but adequate standard before. *FCC v. RCA Communications, Inc.*, 346 U. S. 86, 346 U. S. 90 (1953); *National Broadcasting Co. v. United States*, 319 U. S. 190, 319 U. S. 216-217 (1943); *FCC v. Pottsville Broadcasting Co.*, 309 U. S. 134, 309 U. S. 138 (1940); *FRC v. Nelson Bros. Bond & Mortgage Co.*, 289 U. S. 266, 289 U. S. 285 (1933). We cannot say that the FCC's declaratory ruling in *Red Lion*, or the regulations at issue in *RTNDA*, are beyond the scope of the congressionally conferred power to assure that stations are operated by those whose possession of a license serves "the public interest."

III

The broadcasters challenge the fairness doctrine and its specific manifestations in the personal attack and political editorial rules on conventional First Amendment grounds, alleging that the rules abridge their freedom of speech and press. Their contention is that the First Amendment protects their desire to use their allotted frequencies continuously to broadcast whatever they choose, and to exclude whomever they choose from ever using that frequency. No man may be prevented from saying or publishing what he thinks, or from refusing in his speech or other utterances to give equal weight to the views of his opponents. This right, they say, applies equally to broadcasters.

A

Although broadcasting is clearly a medium affected by a First Amendment interest, *United States v. Paramount Pictures, Inc.*, 334 U. S. 131, 334 U. S. 166 (1948), differences in the characteristics of new media justify differences in the First Amendment standards applied to them.[15] *Joseph Burstyn, Inc. v. Wilson*, 343 U. S. 495, 343 U. S. 503 (1352). For example, the ability of new technology to produce sounds more raucous than those of the human voice justifies restrictions on the sound level, and on the hours and places of use, of sound trucks so long as the restrictions are reasonable and applied without discrimination. *Kovacs v. Cooper*, 336 U. S. 77 (1949).

Just as the Government may limit the use of sound-amplifying equipment potentially so noisy that it drowns out civilized private speech, so may the Government limit the use of broadcast equipment. The right of free speech of a broadcaster, the user of a sound truck, or any other individual does not embrace a right to snuff out the free speech of others. *Associated Press v. United States*, 326 U. S. 1, 326 U. S. 20 (1945).

When two people converse face to face, both should not speak at once if either is to be clearly understood. But the range of the human voice is so limited that there could be meaningful communications if half the people in the United States were talking and the other half listening. Just as clearly, half the people might publish and the other half read. But the reach of radio signals is incomparably greater than the range of the human voice, and the problem of interference is a massive reality. The lack of know-how and equipment may keep many from the air, but only a tiny fraction of those with resources and intelligence can hope to communicate by radio at the same time if intelligible communication is to be had, even if the entire radio spectrum is utilized in the present state of commercially acceptable technology.

It was this fact, and the chaos which ensued from permitting anyone to use any frequency at whatever power level he wished, which made necessary the enactment of the Radio Act of 1927 and the Communications Act of 1934,[16] as the Court has noted at length before. *National Broadcasting Co. v. United States*, 319 U. S. 190, 319 U. S. 210-214 (1943). It was this reality which, at the very least, necessitated first the division of the radio spectrum into portions reserved respectively for public broadcasting and for other important radio uses such as amateur operation, aircraft, police, defense, and navigation, and then the subdivision of each portion, and assignment of specific frequencies to individual users or groups of users. Beyond this, however, because the frequencies reserved for public broadcasting were limited in number, it was essential for the Government to tell some applicants that they could not broadcast at all, because there was room for only a few.

Where there are substantially more individuals who want to broadcast than there are frequencies to allocate, it is idle to posit an unabridgeable First Amendment right to broadcast comparable to the right of every individual to speak, write, or publish. If 100 persons want broadcast licenses, but there are only 10 frequencies to allocate, all of them may have the same "right" to a license, but, if there is to be any effective communication by radio, only a few can be licensed, and the rest must be barred from the airwaves. It would be strange if the First Amendment, aimed at protecting and furthering communications, prevented the Government from making radio communication possible by requiring licenses to broadcast and by limiting the number of licenses so as not to overcrowd the spectrum.

This has been the consistent view of the Court. Congress unquestionably has the power to grant and deny licenses and to eliminate existing stations. *FRC v. Nelson Bros. Bond & Mortgage Co.*, 289 U. S. 266 (1933). No one has a First Amendment right to a license or to monopolize a radio frequency; to deny a station license because "the public interest" requires it "is not a denial of free speech."

National Broadcasting Co. v. United States, 319 U. S. 190, 319 U. S. 227 (1943).

By the same token, as far as the First Amendment is concerned, those who are licensed stand no better than those to whom licenses are refused. A license permits broadcasting, but the licensee has no constitutional right to be the one who holds the license or to monopolize a radio frequency to the exclusion of his fellow citizens. There is nothing in the First Amendment which prevents the Government from requiring a licensee to share his frequency with others and to conduct himself as a proxy or fiduciary with obligations to present those views and voices which are representative of his community and which would otherwise, by necessity, be barred from the airwaves.

This is not to say that the First Amendment is irrelevant to public broadcasting. On the contrary, it has a major role to play, as the Congress itself recognized in § 326, which forbids FCC interference with "the right of free speech by means of radio communication." Because of the scarcity of radio frequencies, the Government is permitted to put restraints on licensees in favor of others whose views should be expressed on this unique medium. But the people as a whole retain their interest in free speech by radio and their collective right to have the medium function consistently with the ends and purposes of the First Amendment. It is the right of the viewers and listeners, not the right of the broadcasters, which is paramount. *See FCC v. Sanders Bros. Radio Station*, 309 U. S. 470, 309 U. S. 475 (1940); *FCC v. Allentown Broadcasting Corp.*, 349 U. S. 358, 349 U. S. 361-362 (1955); 2 Z. *Chafee, Government and Mass Communications* 546 (1947). It is the purpose of the First Amendment to preserve an uninhibited marketplace of ideas in which truth will ultimately prevail, rather than to countenance monopolization of that market, whether it be by the Government itself or a private licensee. *Associated Press v. United States*, 326 U. S. 1, 326 U. S. 20 (1945); *New York Times Co. v. Sullivan*, 376 U. S. 254, 376 U. S. 270 (1964); *Abrams v. United States*, 250 U. S. 616, 250 U. S. 630 (1919) (Holmes, J., dissenting). "[S]peech concerning public affairs is more than self-expression; it is the essence of self-government." *Garrison v. Louisiana*, 379 U. S. 64, 379 U. S. 74-75 (1964). *See* Brennan, The Supreme Court and the Meiklejohn Interpretation of the First Amendment, 79 Harv.L.Rev. 1 (1965). It is the right of the public to receive suitable access to social, political, esthetic, moral, and other ideas and experiences which is crucial here. That right may not constitutionally be abridged either by Congress or by the FCC.

B

Rather than confer frequency monopolies on a relatively small number of licensees, in a Nation of 200,000,000, the Government could surely have decreed that each frequency should be shared among all or some of those who wish to use it, each being assigned a portion of the broadcast day or the broadcast week. The ruling and regulations at issue here do not go quite so far. They assert that, under specified circumstances, a licensee must offer to make available a reasonable amount of broadcast time to those who have a view different from that which has already been expressed on his station. The expression of a political endorsement, or of a personal attack while dealing with a controversial public issue, simply triggers this time-sharing. As we have said, the First Amendment confers no right on licensees to prevent others from broadcasting on "their" frequencies, and no right to an unconditional monopoly of a scarce resource which the Government has denied others the right to use.

In terms of constitutional principle, and as enforced sharing of a scarce resource, the personal attack and political editorial rules are indistinguishable from the equal time provision of § 315, a specific enactment of Congress requiring stations to set aside reply time under specified circumstances and to which the fairness doctrine and these constituent regulations are important complements. That provision, which has been part of the law since 1927, Radio Act of 1927, § 18, 44 Stat. 1170, has been held valid by this Court as an obligation of the licensee relieving him of any power in any way to prevent or censor the broadcast, and thus insulating him from liability for defamation. The constitutionality of the statute under the First Amendment was unquestioned.[17] *Farmers Educ. & Coop. Union v. WDAY*, 360 U. S. 525 (1959).

Nor can we say that it is inconsistent with the First Amendment goal of producing an informed public capable of conducting its own affairs to require a broadcaster to permit answers to personal attacks occurring in the course of discussing controversial issues, or to require that the political opponents of those endorsed by the station be given a chance to communicate with the public.[18] Otherwise, station owners and a few networks would have unfettered power to make time available only to the highest bidders, to communicate only their own views on public issues, people and candidates, and to permit on the air only those with whom they agreed. There is no sanctuary in the

First Amendment for unlimited private censorship operating in a medium not open to all.

"Freedom of the press from governmental interference under the First Amendment does not sanction repression of that freedom by private interests."

"*Associated Press v. United States*, 326 U. S. 1, 326 U. S. 20 (1945)."

C

It is strenuously argued, however, that, if political editorials or personal attacks will trigger an obligation in broadcasters to afford the opportunity for expression to speakers who need not pay for time and whose views are unpalatable to the licensees, then broadcasters will be irresistibly forced to self-censorship, and their coverage of controversial public issues will be eliminated, or at least rendered wholly ineffective. Such a result would indeed be a serious matter, for, should licensees actually eliminate their coverage of controversial issues, the purposes of the doctrine would be stifled.

At this point, however, as the Federal Communications Commission has indicated, that possibility is, at best, speculative. The communications industry, and, in particular, the networks, have taken pains to present controversial issues in the past, and even now they do not assert that they intend to abandon their efforts in this regard.[19] It would be better if the FCC's encouragement were never necessary to induce the broadcasters to meet their responsibility. And if experience with the administration of these doctrines indicates that they have the net effect of reducing, rather than enhancing, the volume and quality of coverage, there will be time enough to reconsider the constitutional implications. The fairness doctrine in the past has had no such overall effect.

That this will occur now seems unlikely, however, since, if present licensees should suddenly prove timorous, the Commission is not powerless to insist that they give adequate and fair attention to public issues.

It does not violate the First Amendment to treat licensees given the privilege of using scarce radio frequencies as proxies for the entire community, obligated to give suitable time and attention to matters of great public concern. To condition the granting or renewal of licenses on a willingness to present representative community views on controversial issues is consistent with the ends and purposes of those constitutional provisions forbidding the abridgment of freedom of speech and freedom of the press. Congress need not stand idly by and permit those with licenses to ignore the problems which beset the people or to exclude from the airways anything but their own views of fundamental questions. The statute, long administrative practice, and cases are to this effect.

Licenses to broadcast do not confer ownership of designated frequencies, but only the temporary privilege of using them. 47 U.S.C. § 301. Unless renewed, they expire within three years. 47 U.S.C. § 307(d). The statute mandates the issuance of licenses if the "public convenience, interest, or necessity will be served thereby." 47 U.S.C. § 307(a). In applying this standard, the Commission for 40 years has been choosing licensees based in part on their program proposals. In *FRC v. Nelson Bros. Bond & Mortgage Co.*, 289 U. S. 266, 289 U. S. 279 (1933), the Court noted that, in "view of the limited number of available broadcasting frequencies, the Congress has authorized allocation and licenses." In determining how best to allocate frequencies, the Federal Radio Commission considered the needs of competing communities and the programs offered by competing stations to meet those needs; moreover, if needs or programs shifted, the Commission could alter its allocations to reflect those shifts. *Id.* at 289 U. S. 285. In the same vein, in *FCC v. Pottsville Broadcasting Co.*, 309 U. S. 134, 309 U. S. 137-138 (1940), the Court noted that the statutory standard was a supple instrument to effect congressional desires "to maintain . . . a grip on the dynamic aspects of radio transmission" and allay fears that, "in the absence of governmental control, the public interest might be subordinated to monopolistic domination in the broadcasting field." Three years later, the Court considered the validity of the Commission's chain broadcasting regulations, which, among other things, forbade stations from devoting too much time to network programs in order that there be suitable opportunity for local programs serving local needs. The Court upheld the regulations, unequivocally recognizing that the Commission was more than a traffic policeman concerned with the technical aspects of broadcasting and that it neither exceeded its powers under the statute nor transgressed the First Amendment in interesting itself in general program format and the kinds of programs broadcast by licensees. *National Broadcasting Co. v. United States*, 319 U. S. 190 (1943).

D

The litigants embellish their First Amendment arguments

with the contention that the regulations are so vague that their duties are impossible to discern. Of this point it is enough to say that, judging the validity of the regulations on their face as they are presented here, we cannot conclude that the FCC has been left a free hand to vindicate its own idiosyncratic conception of the public interest or of the requirements of free speech. Past adjudications by the FCC give added precision to the regulations; there was nothing vague about the FCC's specific ruling in *Red Lion* that Fred Cook should be provided an opportunity to reply. The regulations at issue in *RTNDA* could be employed in precisely the same way as the fairness doctrine was in *Red Lion*. Moreover, the FCC itself has recognized that the applicability of its regulations to situations beyond the scope of past cases may be questionable, 32 Fed.Reg. 10303, 10304 and n. 6, and will not impose sanctions in such cases without warning. We need not approve every aspect of the fairness doctrine to decide these cases, and we will not now pass upon the constitutionality of these regulations by envisioning the most extreme applications conceivable, *United States v. Sullivan*, 332 U. S. 689, 332 U. S. 694 (1948), but will deal with those problems if and when they arise.

We need not and do not now ratify every past and future decision by the FCC with regard to programming. There is no question here of the Commission's refusal to permit the broadcaster to carry a particular program or to publish his own views; of a discriminatory refusal to require the licensee to broadcast certain views which have been denied access to the airwaves; of government censorship of a particular program contrary to § 326; or of the official government view dominating public broadcasting. Such questions would raise more serious First Amendment issues. But we do hold that the Congress and the Commission do not violate the First Amendment when they require a radio or television station to give reply time to answer personal attacks and political editorials.

E

It is argued that, even if, at one time, the lack of available frequencies for all who wished to use them justified the Government's choice of those who would best serve the public interest by acting as proxy for those who would present differing views, or by giving the latter access directly to broadcast facilities, this condition no longer prevails, so that continuing control is not justified. To this there are several answers.

Scarcity is not entirely a thing of the past. Advances in technology, such as microwave transmission, have led to more efficient utilization of the frequency spectrum, but uses for that spectrum have also gown apace.[20] Portions of the spectrum must be reserved for vital uses unconnected with human communication, such as radionavigational aids used by aircraft and vessels. Conflicts have even emerged between such vital functions as defense preparedness and experimentation in methods of averting mid-air collisions through radio warning devices.[21] "Land mobile services" such as police, ambulance, fire department, public utility, and other communications systems have been occupying an increasingly crowded portion of the frequency spectrum,[22] and there are, apart from licensed amateur radio operators' equipment, 5,000,000 transmitters operated on the "citizens' band," which is also increasingly congested.[23] Among the various uses for radio frequency space, including marine, aviation, amateur, military, and common carrier users, there are easily enough claimants to permit use of the whole with an even smaller allocation to broadcast radio and television uses than now exists.

Comparative hearings between competing applicants for broadcast spectrum space are by no means a thing of the past. The radio spectrum has become so congested that, at times, it has been necessary to suspend new applications.[24] The very high frequency television spectrum is, in the country's major markets, almost entirely occupied, although space reserved for ultra high frequency television transmission, which is a relatively recent development as a commercially viable alternative, has not yet been completely filled.[25]

The rapidity with which technological advances succeed one another to create more efficient use of spectrum space, on the one hand, and to create new uses for that space by ever-growing numbers of people, on the other, makes it unwise to speculate on the future allocation of that space. It is enough to say that the resource is one of considerable and growing importance whose scarcity impelled its regulation by an agency authorized by Congress. Nothing in this record, or in our own researches, convinces us that the resource is no longer one for which there are more immediate and potential uses than can be accommodated, and for which wise planning is essential.[26] This does not mean, of course, that every possible wavelength must be occupied at every hour by some vital use in order to sustain the congressional judgment. The substantial capital investment required for many uses, in addition to the potentiality for confusion and interference inherent in any scheme for continuous kaleidoscopic reallocation of all available space may make this unfeasible. The allocation need not be made at such a break-neck pace that the objectives of the allocation are themselves imperiled.[27]

Even where there are gaps in spectrum utilization, the fact remains that existing broadcasters have often attained their present position because of their initial government selection in competition with others before new technological advances opened new opportunities for further uses. Long experience in broadcasting, confirmed habits of listeners and viewers, network affiliation, and other advantages in program procurement give existing broadcasters a substantial advantage over new entrants, even where new entry is technologically possible. These advantages are the fruit of a preferred position conferred by the Government. Some present possibility for new entry by competing stations is not enough, in itself, to render unconstitutional the Government's effort to assure that a broadcaster's programming ranges widely enough to serve the public interest.

In view of the scarcity of broadcast frequencies, the Government's role in allocating those frequencies, and the legitimate claims of those unable without governmental assistance to gain access to those frequencies for expression of their views, we hold the regulations and ruling at issue here are both authorized by statute and constitutional.[28] The judgment of the Court of Appeals in *Red Lion* is affirmed and that in *RTNDA* reversed, and the causes remanded for proceedings consistent with this opinion.

It is so ordered.

Not having heard oral argument in these cases, MR. JUSTICE DOUGLAS took no part in the Court's decision.

* Together with No. 717, *United States et al. v. Radio Television News Directors Assn. et al.*, on certiorari to the United States Court of Appeals for the Seventh Circuit, argued April 3, 1969.

1. Do you think the Fairness Doctrine, which required broadcast companies to give both sides of public issues equal air time, helped prevent media bias?

2. The Fairness Doctrine was eliminated in 1987. Do you think that, if revived, the Fairness Doctrine would help prevent media bias in the twenty-first century? What would you change about the doctrine if you were to reinstate it today?

CHAPTER 4

WHAT ADVOCACY ORGANIZATIONS SAY

Those who work to protect the media from undue influence from the government have long been watching the news to ensure the First Amendment isn't violated. But they also watch and read to make sure that the media is being honest and fair. Watchdogs look at who owns the outlets, which pundits and talking heads are interviewed when an expert opinion is required, and even the words outlets choose when telling a story. Organizations that monitor the media look at preventing not just a particular spin, but any biased perspective at all, in an effort to maintain the integrity of the media. As you read their takes on the issue, you'll explore what professional news consumers think of media bias and how they believe the issue can be handled going forward.

"I PLAY AN OBJECTIVE EXPERT ON TV," BY JULIE HOLLAR, FROM *OTHERWORDS*, MARCH 1, 2010

SCORES OF PUNDITS APPEARING ON TELEVISION NEWS ARE ACTUALLY PAID CORPORATE LOBBYISTS AND PUBLIC RELATIONS PROS.

When you're cruising past the cable news channels, do you ever find yourself wondering who are those folks pontificating on TV chat shows? A new investigation provides some answers—along with lots of questions about what the cable channels are hiding from viewers.

Scores of pundits appearing on Fox News, CNN, MSNBC, and other networks are actually paid corporate lobbyists and public relations pros. Shamefully, the networks don't disclose their corporate ties to us, the audience. Reporter Sebastian Jones recently revealed in *The Nation* magazine that at least 75 registered lobbyists, public relations representatives, and corporate executives have appeared on the cable networks since 2007, with no disclosure that they're being paid by companies and industries to boost them. Some of these stealth corporate pundits are regulars. They've appeared hundreds of times on TV over the past three years.

For example, during insurance giant AIG's collapse—and its ensuing massive government bailout— some pundits brought on to discuss the story were, unbeknownst to viewers, actually working for AIG, as lobbyists or public relations advisers. An MSNBC segment on job creation featured one guest strongly urging Obama to build more nuclear plants. Viewers should have been told that this "expert" happened to sit on the board of a major nuclear power company.

And as the health-care debate unfolded throughout the past year, a number of pundits and former lawmakers have made numerous appearances to talk about health insurance reform—all the while employed or bankrolled by insurance and pharmaceutical companies.

In almost every case, viewers had no way of knowing these guests' affiliations.

This isn't the first time we've learned that there's often something fishy about these so-called "experts." In 2008, *The New York Times* broke the story that the Pentagon had been feeding talking points to TV military analysts who were cited across national cable, network TV, and radio broadcasts. In the lead-up to the Iraq War, the Pentagon recruited over 75 retired generals to act as "message force multipliers" to support the war. They received special Pentagon briefings and talking points that the analysts would often parrot on national television, even when, the *Times* reported, "they suspected the information was false or inflated."

Most of these "analysts" also had ties to military contractors who stood to benefit from the analysts' on-air assessments. The military analysts themselves told the Times that "the networks asked few questions about their outside business interests," and "were only dimly aware" of the special Pentagon briefings they were receiving.

Some networks have written policies demanding that contributors and analysts reveal their conflicts of interest. But it's hard to take those guidelines very seriously. As Jones points out in his *Nation* article, one MSNBC official suggested that their idea of disclosure might be to post relevant information about their guests on the MSNBC website. That's not going to be much help to the hundreds of thousands of people watching these PR pundits on TV.

In a media system already dominated by official sources from government and big business, why are cable channels relying on paid spokespeople and lobbyists as commentators? And why are these channels hiding the affiliations of their pundits?

Columnist Jim Hightower once suggested that politicians should be forced to wear the corporate logos of their major contributors. That idea just gets better with age, but how about we do the same with these ubiquitous TV pundits? Join us at FAIR to demand answers and accountability. Sign our petition at FAIR.org to MSNBC, Fox News, CNN, CNBC and Fox Business Channel, demanding that they come clean about their corporate-sponsored pundits. In the meantime, crank up the skepticism every time you turn on the tube.

Julie Hollar is the managing editor of Extra!, *the magazine of Fairness & Accuracy In Reporting (FAIR).*

1. Hollar explores the idea that media bias comes not only from what the reporters say, but the sources they choose. Do you think that the "talking heads" the media relies on to discuss

ideas are used to forward certain outlets' biases? Explain why or why not.

2. If you had to book an expert to discuss a particular idea, how would you choose your guest to prevent showing a bias? What are things you would look for to make sure your guest is the best possible person to present the information you need?

"POLITICAL BIAS SATURATES EGYPT'S MEDIA," FROM INTERNATIONAL MEDIA SUPPORT, AUGUST 20, 2013

THE EGYPTIAN MEDIA'S COVERAGE OF THE PAST WEEKS' CONFRONTATIONS BETWEEN THE COUNTRY'S NEW MILITARY BACKED GOVERNMENT AND THE MUSLIM BROTHERHOOD HAS BEEN "SATURATED WITH CLEAR POLITICAL BIAS AND REFLECTS THE CURRENT POLITICAL DIVISION," SAYS MICHAEL IRVING JENSEN, HEAD OF IMS' MIDDLE EAST AND NORTH AFRICA DEPARTMENT

The majority of Egypt's mass media, including both state and private media, has embarked on a new discourse in which they portray the supporters of ousted President Mohamed Morsi as terrorists.

Also media outlets affiliated with the Muslim Brotherhood display a clear lack of professional standards, and both sides of the media have been accused of provoking public violence.

"It is of paramount importance that Egypt's media adhere to journalistic standards and provide their audiences with non-partisan, professional coverage, in order to avoid inflaming the situation further," adds Michael Irving Jensen.

POLARISED COVERAGE

Since the crackdown on pro-Morsi protests began, state TV has provided little coverage of accusations raised against police officers from Western media and human rights groups.

State-run media and some private TV outlets are fiercely anti-Morsi, stressing that his supporters are armed and have caused casualties among the police.

TV stations affiliated with the Muslim Brotherhood, on the other hand, reserve their anger for the army, emphasising deaths among the protesters and showing gruesome pictures of the dead and wounded.

According to the BBC, TV stations affiliated with the Muslim Brotherhood, Ahrar 25 and Al-Shar'iyah were broadcasting live from the Rabaa al-Adawiya camp, one of the principal areas of pro-Morsi demonstrations. The feeds showed intensely emotional and rousing speeches delivered by Islamists addressing the demonstrators. Video of protesters in the camp was broadcast alongside clips showing piles of dead bodies and several charred carcasses.

State TV stations Channel One and Nile News, as well as the private channels ON TV and CBC, were also broadcasting live footage of the clearance of pro-Morsi camps. Contrary to the broadcasts from pro-Morsi channels they were highly critical of the demonstrators, claiming that they were armed and have killed several members of the security forces. Broadcasts of the events from state TV show a banner in English in the upper left corner reading: "Egypt Fights Terrorism".

JOURNALISTS UNDER SEVERE PRESSURE

According to the Committee to Protect Journalists and Reporters without Borders, three journalists have been confirmed killed since August 14.

The Egyptian human rights group Association for Freedom of Thought and Expression (AFTE) reported 32 separate violations against local journalists, including assaults, detentions or confiscation of press equipment. Reporters without Borders report at least 15 journalists, both Egyptian and foreign, have had their rights violated through attacks, seizure of equipment, or detention.

"The Egyptian authorities must send a clear signal that journalists cannot be harmed or harassed as they attempt to cover the unrest. If the authorities genuinely want to establish democracy, it is key that they tolerate all viewpoints", says IMS' Michael Irving Jensen.

With independent journalism under pressure, providing an alternative to the current discourse is a key challenge for Lina Attalah, editor-in-chief at the

English-language Mada Masr website, she said to the online magazine Jadaliyya on Friday:

"How can one remain autonomous and sustainable, to survive, grow and show that there is an alternative possible journalism? This is what we are grappling with right now and I hope we will have some good answers."

1. State-run media will always be biased toward the state. Do you think these sorts of outlets, as exist in places like Egypt, can be trusted to deliver accurate news about what the government is doing? Explain what news you might trust from a government news source and what news the bias might negatively affect.

2. The article discusses how both state-run and private media played live coverage of political demonstrations, but with different footage. Would you be more likely to believe that live footage is accurately portraying an event? How would you go about framing a live event for different sides if you could only show live footage?

"SENATOR'S INQUIRY INTO FACEBOOK'S EDITORIAL DECISIONS RUNS AFOUL OF THE FIRST AMENDMENT," BY SOPHIA COPE, FROM THE ELECTRONIC FREEDOM FOUNDATION, MAY 18, 2016

Allegations that Facebook's "trending" news stories are not actually those that are most popular among users drew the attention of Sen. John Thune (R-SD), who sent a letter of inquiry to Facebook suggesting that the company may be "misleading" the public, and demanding to know details about how the company decides what content to display in the trending news feed. Sen. Thune appears particularly disturbed by charges that the company routinely excludes news stories of interest to conservative readers.

Congressional inquiries usually come with the tacit understanding that Congress investigates when it thinks it could also legislate. Yet any legislative action in response to the revelations would run afoul of the First Amendment. It is possible that Sen. Thune, as chairman of the Senate Commerce Committee, sees Facebook as engaging is "unfair or deceptive" trade practices, but that still does not create a legal basis for regulating what amounts to Facebook's editorial decision-making.

FIRST AMENDMENT PROTECTS FACEBOOK'S EDITORIAL DECISIONS

In *Miami Herald Publishing Co. v. Tornillo* (1974), the Supreme Court held that under the First Amendment, the government may not tell a private publisher what to print or not to print, nor may the government punish a publisher for making editorial decisions. The Court stated:

> The choice of material to go into a newspaper, and the decisions made as to limitations on the size and content of the paper, and treatment of public issues and public officials—whether fair or unfair—constitute the exercise of editorial control and judgment.

Although that case involved a newspaper, the constitutional rule is just as applicable to the Internet, where a wide range of websites—from newspapers' digital homes to social media platforms native to the online space—have the right to be free from government interference with their publishing practices.

Even if Congress never takes any action, Sen. Thune's letter alone—questioning Facebook's editorial decisions—is an improper intrusion into editorial freedom. Moreover, such an official government inquiry into constitutionally protected activity can create a "chilling effect" that dissuades individuals, even companies, from acting in wholly legal ways.

Sen. Thune's letter is a close cousin to the tactic deployed by the sheriff of Cook County, Illinois, who wrote letters on official letterhead urging credit card companies to stop providing payment processing services to classifieds websites like Backpage.com, while suggesting that the companies might be legally culpable if they refused to heed the sheriff's request. Backpage challenged the sheriff's actions and the Seventh Circuit Court of Appeals held that the sheriff violated the website's First Amendment rights.

As a Republican, Sen. Thune seems offended that Facebook might be purposefully excluding conservative news stories. But conservatives were outraged when the FCC proposed conducting a newsroom survey in 2014. Republican lawmakers and conservative commentators complained that the Obama administration was maneuvering to control media content in violation of the First Amendment. And Sen. Thune himself, in 2007, criticized those in Washington, DC, who, he said, were "reviving an old idea that the government can, and should, regulate the reporting of news, information and ideas."

FACEBOOK SHOULD BE FAIR AND TRANSPARENT ABOUT ITS CONTENT POLICIES

There is a distinction that we want to emphasize: Facebook as a curator of news stories—exercising editorial judgment just like any other media outlet—and Facebook as a social media platform and host of user-generated content.

As a legal matter, in both roles, Facebook is protected by the First Amendment and thus has a right to publish content online free from government interference. As a policy matter, however, it would behoove the company to be more transparent about its content policies.

While it is understandable that Facebook users might want more transparency about what goes into producing the "trending" news feed (including whether the company is exercising political bias), we are more concerned about how Facebook acts in its more prominent role as a host of user-generated content.

As a social media platform, Facebook solicits and displays often highly personal text and images that individuals post to express themselves and connect with their loved ones and communities. People around the world have come to significantly rely on Facebook, even in life-and-death situations.

Yet the company reorders, emphasizes and minimizes posts to everyone's news feed. And it enforces its terms of service in a selective manner: deleting some posts, censoring some images, and throwing some users off its service, while letting other apparent offenders go unpunished. We have criticized Facebook for unclear content policies and arbitrary enforcement of its terms of service.

At onlinecensorship.org, EFF is tracking such behavior by private social media companies. Whether a company justifies its actions by referencing its terms of service or some other reason, we want to better understand patterns in social media censorship. We encourage individuals who have had their own content removed or their account suspended to report their experiences there.

Facebook has a right to make its own decisions about what it does or does not say online. But it when it comes to providing a service that enables others to speak as well, Facebook should be fair and transparent about how it handles other people's content—and the company should always expect to have its decisions explored and debated by its users and the wider public.

1. Facebook was accused of hiding conservative news stories, which some perceived as an example of media bias. Although Facebook is merely a social

networking site that does not produce its own original content, do you think that its behavior should be viewed as media bias? Should companies like Facebook, where a number of people get their news, be held to the same standards as traditional media companies?

2. If you're going to rely on social media for news, what are some steps you can take to make sure you're seeing a mix of stories? Should you expect to get nonbiased stories from social media, or do you think you need to carefully choose which outlets to follow in order to combat only seeing news that meets your own bias?

"THE TRUTH'S LIBERAL TILT," BY JASON SALZMAN, FROM *OTHERWORDS*, MAY 21, 2012

There's no media bias in citing facts about Obama's record.

When you ask conservatives for proof of the "liberal media bias" they are so concerned about, you often get a response along the lines of, "The media are liberal because we say so! It's obvious."

So I was happy to find a case where the familiar band of conservatives was saying they had actual proof, hard evidence, of how the media favors the other side over their own.

Their evidence? An introduction to a speech by President Barack Obama.

William Dean Singleton, the outgoing chairman of the Associated Press, introduced Obama prior to a recent speech before hundreds of journalists in Washington.

"He inherited the headwinds of the worst economic recession since the Great Depression," Singleton said. "He pushed through Congress the biggest economic recovery plan in history and led a government reorganization of two of the big three auto manufacturers to save them from oblivion. He pursued domestic and foreign-policy agendas that were controversial to many, highlighted by his signature into law of the most comprehensive health care legislation in history. And the budget plans proposed by the president on the one hand, and Republicans on the other hand, aren't even on the same planet."

Do you see anything so offensive in what Singleton said? All I see is facts.

Yes, there was big recession. Yes, he saved two of three auto companies. Yes, his agenda was controversial and distinct from the GOP agenda. And yes, his economic recovery plan was one of the biggest in U.S. history.

Everything Singleton said was factual. It may be true that he wasn't being balanced, but Mitt Romney was on deck to address the same group of journalists the next day.

Besides, are you really going to recite the leader of the free world's failures after he's doing you the favor of speaking to your luncheon? That's rude.

But conservative media critics saw Singleton's introduction as evidence of the liberal bias that they see everywhere in professional journalism, from *The New York Times* to CBS News and beyond.

"I'm surprised Singleton wasn't wearing an Obama button," Fox News' Bill O'Reilly said about Singleton's introduction. "I mean, come on. The president understands that most in the media will back him."

Conservative *Washington Times* columnist Charles Hurt wrote that Singleton sang Obama "an icky love song in which he reminisced about all their hot dates and then pledged his undying love forever." Actually, Singleton told anecdotes about Obama speaking at previous luncheons.

Not to be outdone, talk-radio host Rush Limbaugh told listeners that the AP's CEO "stood up and just lauded Obama as one of the greatest human beings ever, one of the greatest presidents ever, one of the greatest quotes ever, one of the greatest guys ever."

Singleton ended his introduction of Obama by saying that these days "the only thing anyone seems willing to compromise on is….well, I can't think of anything."

Here's a suggestion, and it goes out to conservatives and progressives alike:

Let's agree to acknowledge the facts.

When a journalist says something like Obama saved two of the three big U.S. automakers and he came into office during the worst recession since the Great Depression, let's not cry media bias.

Let's call those facts and honor them as such, so we can have an honest debate about what we truly disagree on.

A former media critic for the Rocky Mountain News, *Jason Salzman is board chair of Rocky Mountain Media Watch and author of* Making the News: A Guide for Activists and Nonprofits.

1. Do you think that what the Associated Press did, praising President Obama in an introduction at an event it hosted, shows a bias? Or do you think, as the author does, that because the praise was grounded in facts that it is not a biased statement?

2. What sort of interaction should the press and the government have? How can the media work with the politicians they cover without becoming biased toward one party or the other?

"THE EFFECTS OF FACT-CHECKING," BY KELLY BORN, FROM THE WILLIAM & FLORA HEWLETT FOUNDATION, APRIL 28, 2015

Fact-checking is everywhere, but does it have any impact? This was one of my biggest questions coming out of an American Press Institute (API) conference I attended in Washington this past January.

The growth of fact-checking is indisputable: The number of fact-checking stories—from groups like Factcheck, FactChecker (home of the "Pinocchios"), and Politifact—increased by more than 50% between 2004 and 2008. From 2008 to 2012, they grew by more than 300%.

But are those stories having any effect? Three new studies just came out—overseen by API, and supported by the Hewlett Foundation, along with our colleagues at the Democracy Fund and the Rita Allen Foundation. One of these, Estimating Fact-checking's Effects—from Brendan Nyhan of Dartmouth College and Jason Reifler of the University of Exeter—gets precisely at this question of impact. Here's what I found to be some of the study's most interesting findings:

First, views on fact-checking's "favorability" ratings differ depending on political party affiliation. While the views of "low-knowledge" respondents don't differ much depending on whether they are Republicans or Democrats (29% vs 36% view fact-checking favorably, respectively), it makes a real difference for people with high levels of political knowledge: "just 34% of Republicans ... have very favorable views of fact-checkers compared with 59% of high-knowledge Democrats." Nyhan and Reifler hypothesize that this may be due to Republicans / conservatives tendency to "hold less favorable opinions of the news media" overall, coupled with a greater likelihood to believe that there is a liberal media bias.

Then they looked at impact. Here there were (at least) two big questions:

Belief Accuracy: One risk inherent in fact-checking stories is that "exposing people to false claims in an effort to debunk them" can lead to a situation where readers recall the misinformation more clearly than they remember the intended correction. Here the question is: Does exposure to fact-checking content increase "belief accuracy?" Nyhan and Reifler found, through post-exposure surveys, that "the rate of correct answers increased from 12% to 19% among people with low political knowledge," and was even more effective among people with "high political knowledge" (from 22% to 32%).

Motivated Reasoning: Many experimental studies in psychology and political science have found that new factual information doesn't necessarily change erroneous, pre-existing beliefs. In fact, it can actually backfire for some groups (e.g., depending on the issue, context, and messenger, counterfactual information can cause partisans to more deeply entrench in their pre-existing beliefs). Thus Nyhan and Reifler expected partisans to be more likely to learn/recall "belief-consistent" facts.

- True to their hypothesis, the researchers found that corrections of inaccurate statements are more persuasive when the reader and politician belong to the same political parties. "Readers tend to think the opposing party politician's statement was false, even before they read the correction." This suggests that fact-checking may be particularly important during primary contests (though fact-checking is currently more common during general elections).
- Contrary to their expectations, they found that "correct answers increased somewhat more for belief-inconsistent facts (from 9% to 20%) than for belief-consistent facts (from 14% to 22%)."

- "Republican knowledge of belief-inconsistent facts increased by five percentage points and by ten percentage points for belief-consistent ones. The pattern for Democrats is the opposite, however — knowledge increased by 15 percentage points for belief-inconsistent facts compared with eight percentage points for belief-consistent facts."

It's worth noting that the public at large is not the only potential audience for fact-checking, nor necessarily even the most important one. In a prior article, Nyhan also explored the impact of increased fact-checking on politicians' behaviors—that is, testing whether there's a deterrent effect.

In a 2014 study of 1,200 legislators in nine states, Nyhan and Reifler sent candidates and policymakers reminders about "the risks to their reputation and electoral security if they are caught making questionable statements." The result? A 55% reduction in the likelihood of receiving a negative PolitiFact rating, or having the accuracy of their statements questioned publicly, in comparison to legislators who were not sent reminders. That said, state legislators are very seldom fact-checked, anyway, and it's not clear whether the same effect would hold for Congress.

Nevertheless, fact-checking seems to me a promising development in the journalistic field. For it to succeed, newsrooms (and, when relevant, funders) still need to wrestle with questions like when and what to fact-check in order to maintain both relevance and bipartisan credibility, how to scale the reach of existing efforts, and whether and how to expand beyond fact-checking politicians and pundits to other purveyors of misinformation. But those are topics for another day. For now, I'll just say I'm grateful to API and all the researchers we're supporting—and excited for the next round of research releases!

1. Do you think, as the study finds, that hearing about media bias and fact-checking will make you remember the false or biased fact more than the true, unbiased fact? What can you do to help combat this mental bias against the new information you've received?

2. People are more likely to believe a fact-checking story if the new information aligns with their existing beliefs or if they belong to the same political party as the person disputing the initial fact. How can media fact-checkers present their information in a way that will appeal to readers of all political affiliations? Are there sources you would use or avoid when fact-checking the news to make sure the accurate facts are presented in a way that is believable to all readers?

CHAPTER 5

WHAT THE MEDIA SAY

The media is its own biggest critic, and nothing proves that more than the number of journalists and editors who write about the media and its shortcomings. From online news sites critiquing mainstream print media to print journalists debating the merits of television news events, in this chapter you'll take a look at what reporters and writers have to say about their colleagues and how they view the problem of media bias from inside the media. They'll explore the many particulars of media bias and the ways in which the media can work better to fight their bias when reporting the news. You'll also be asked to consider the bias that could be seen in the analysis of media bias and what that means for the media.

"TIME MAGAZINE'S LATEST COVER STORY IS FULL ON PROPAGANDA," BY ALICE SALLES, FROM *THE ANTIMEDIA*, OCTOBER 7, 2016

Time magazine's parent company is a top donor to Hillary Clinton's presidential campaign — a factor that may help explain the publication's obsession with blaming Russian president Vladimir Putin for "rigging" the U.S. presidential election.

This year, alone, Time Inc., the organization behind *Time* — one of the most prestigious American weekly news magazines in history — donated nearly $15,000 to the Clinton campaign. A second organization, Time Warner, which was deeply tied to *Time* until 2014, is also a major Clinton fan. The company gave her campaign $327,308 in individual contributions in 2016, alone.

But perhaps most telling of the organization's preferences is the presence of Nancy Gibbs as *Time*'s managing editor. At the tender age of 53, she *"shattered a glass ceiling"* by taking over for Richard Stengel, who in 2013 *"[stepped] down from his news magazine job to join the Obama administration at the Department of State,"* *Politico* reported.

Gibbs is a competent writer, whose impressive resume includes writing for *Time* for 28 years. This makes her *"one of the most published writers in the history of the magazine, having been an essayist and lead writer on virtually every major news event of the past two decades,"* according to Magazine.org.

But *Time*'s praise for Clinton since Gibbs became managing editor, much like her former colleague Stengel's dedication to President Obama as the Under Secretary of

State for Public Diplomacy and Public Affairs, is also part of her legacy. Gibbs, herself, has praised Clinton in her articles, and on one occasion, she participated in a Clinton Foundation annual meeting.

Keeping that in mind, it's apparent the writers under her watch are likely steered toward writing pieces she would see fit, ignoring facts and reporting hearsay as truth despite a lack of evidence.

The magazine's latest effort to paint Clinton and the DNC's leadership as the victims of media bias comes in the form of a cover piece entitled "How Russia Wants to Undermine the U.S. Election."

Amid reports of electoral fraud perpetrated by the Democratic Party, which places Clinton as the top beneficiary, the story suggests the Obama administration, along with U.S. intelligence and law-enforcement agencies, have *"seen mounting evidence of an active Russian influence operation targeting the 2016 presidential election."* The article does not acknowledge the DNC's own meddling and manipulation.

Admitting "the Russians" would have a hard time *"[swaying] the actual vote count, because our election infrastructure is decentralized and voting machines are not accessible from the Internet,"* *Time*'s Massimo Calabresi argues they may still *"sow disruption and instability up to, and on, Election Day."*

Basing an entire report on testimonials given to *Time* by *"a dozen senior U.S. officials"* who were left unnamed, the piece mostly dwells in metaphysical *"mumbo-jumbo,"* claiming the dangerous Russians could *"[undermine] faith in the result [of the elections] and in democracy itself."* [emphasis added]

Still, Calabresi adds that U.S. officials do not have evidence to support their allegations regarding Russia's role in "rigging the election." Instead, the article suggests that *"while U.S. officials have 'high confidence' that Russia is behind what they describe as a major influence operation, senior U.S. officials tell TIME, their evidence would not yet stand up in court."* He added that the two main hacking groups, believed to be tied to Russian intelligence, prove Russia is involved in rigging the election.

Despite *Time*'s wishful thinking, the only three characteristics officials have used to connect the hackers to Russia are:

"[E]xpensive digital tools, suggesting state sponsorship; an interest in pursuing sensitive, embarrassing or strategically significant information, rather than financially beneficial data; and a choice of targets that align with Russian political objectives."

Further, Calabresi adds, *"U.S. law-enforcement agencies are scrambling to uncover the extent of the Russian operation, counter it and harden the country's election infrastructure."* This is all while *"a murky network of Russian hackers and their associates"* works to *"[step] up the pace of leaks of stolen documents designed to affect public opinion and give the impression that the election is vulnerable, including emails from the computers of the Democratic National Committee (DNC)."* Here, he effectively but subtly ties Julian Assange, the Australian computer programmer, publisher, journalist, and editor-in-chief of the organization he founded, WikiLeaks, to "the Russians."

In an August interview, Assange gave a compelling explanation as to why members of the mainstream U.S. media, who are often backers of Democratic presidential nominees, have repeatedly accused him of being a Russian intelligence plant.

"Everyone accepts that the emails that we published, the 20,000 leaked DNC emails, are accurate. Nobody is saying that they did not say something that was listed in the emails," he told RT.com. Over the past ten years, Assange added, *"WikiLeaks has [had] a perfect … record of never getting it wrong — it is an impressive record and it is the reason why it takes a while before we publish information — because we want to keep that record."*

He continued:

"Given that the real source is known, in this case it is the DNC, it is Debbie Wasserman Schultz, it is Luis Miranda the Communications Director — we know these are their emails so there's quite a difficulty for the Clinton campaign to try to outmaneuver WikiLeaks. The content itself is unquestionable so instead you have to bring in another actor, so they had to bring in Russian intelligence agencies."

Unfortunately for *Time* and its managing editor, these emails, which come from the DNC and its top-ranking officials, *"show the DNC rigged and manipulated the Democratic primary in favor of Hillary Clinton,"* and that is a problem for the Clinton campaign and its narrative.

Instead of discussing these matters — which would all be tied to the story's main theme of "election rigging" — *Time*'s Calabresi chooses to slam Republican presidential candidate Donald Trump for comments made after the DNC leak was publicized.

After being part of a classified intelligence briefing on the Russian "threat," Calabresi admits, Trump said "*nobody knows with definitive certainty that [the hackers behind the DNC leak were] in fact [from] Russia. It may be, but it may also be China, another country or individual.*"

Ignoring the fact the presidential nominee had been part of a classified briefing on the matter, *Time*'s Calabresi still condemns the candidate for choosing not to blame Russia without evidence — again choosing to ignore facts and, instead, using solely speculative arguments to defend his story.

President Obama once mocked 2012 Republican Presidential candidate Mitt Romney for claiming Russia was the biggest geopolitical threat facing America. At the time, Obama hit the candidate by saying:

"*The 1980s are now calling to ask for their foreign policy back because the Cold War's been over for 20 years.*"

Well President Obama, how about that? Ronald Reagan called and asked you to bring that wall down and wipe that smirk off your face. You're now a cold war instigator, and your mouthpieces can't wait for Mrs. Clinton to win. After all, her campaign has already promised to go full force against Syria, prompting the beginning of a conflicting period that could put the United States and Russia on a warpath.

Unless solid proof linking these hacks to Russian intelligence is produced, former National Security

Administration (NSA) contractor and whistleblower Edward Snowden once tweeted, it's hard to believe Russia is behind all this. After all, if the Kremlin were behind it, the NSA would know. And if the NSA knows, why won't it show us proof?

1. The author suggests that because of the cover story *Time* chose, it is showing a clear bias. However, many media organizations also seek to present stories that come from different sides. How can readers of *Time*'s cover story know if the story they're reading is biased or an objective presentation of fact? What would you do if you read the story and didn't believe the premise?

2. The *Time* story discussed in the article relies heavily on unnamed sources, which many people believe should be avoided since it makes it difficult to verify. Do you think using unnamed sources makes a news story inherently biased? If a journalist can't find a source willing to be named, what should they do to make sure they're not expressing a bias with their reporting?

EXCERPT FROM "MIGRANT OR REFUGEE? WHY IT MATTERS WHICH WORD YOU CHOOSE," BY CHARLOTTE TAYLOR, FROM *THE CONVERSATION* WITH THE PARTNERSHIP OF THE UNIVERSITY OF SUSSEX, SEPTEMBER 14, 2015

Across Europe, a debate is raging about how to describe the thousands of people escaping war and turmoil in their own countries and making the journey to safer places. Are they refugees or migrants? The question is important: since European leaders have been justifying inaction over their plight by dismissing many of them as "economic migrants" who are less deserving of help.

Al-Jazeera has made a firm decision on this issue, announcing that it will stop using the umbrella term "migrants" when referring to the refugee crisis in the Mediterranean.

By choosing the term "migrant" over "refugee" (where the latter would be accurate), the choice denies the person their internationally recognised human rights, under the UN Refugee Convention.

But Al-Jazeera also noted that the very meaning of the word "migrant" was changing. What was once a basic description has come to carry negative connotations.

This kind of semantic degrading is common for words relating to controversial topics. We need only think of the endless cycle of terms used to describe people with disabilities, which often develop into insults and are eventually replaced.

In the early stages of a meaning change there is a tendency for people to resist the new interpretation, by claiming that they are using the dictionary definition. But dictionaries do not merely define words – they also describe how they are used. If a negative meaning develops this will be listed. For example, the definition of "villain" has shifted from meaning someone of low-born status "villein", to the current understanding of evil.

LOADED WORDS

At any one moment in time there are a range of terms available to describe human migration. The use of one name over another involves a choice and also carries information about the speaker's opinion towards those they are describing.

For example, when people talk about "expatriates" or "expats", they are often discussing affluent people, who have moved to another country. As Mawuna Remarque Koutonin argues, they are usually from the same country as themselves and often white.

British nationals constitute the second largest group of European foreign born residents in [Spain] (http://ec.europa.eu/eurostat/statistics-explained/index.php/File:Main_countries_of_citizenship_and_birth_of_the_foreign_foreign-born_population,*1_January_2014*(%C2%B9). Most moved there looking for a better quality of life, enabled through the lower cost of living. They are "economic migrants", but this term is not used to describe them in the UK. Instead it is most commonly used to refer to people moving from less affluent countries, both inside and outside the EU.

One way we can demonstrate how terms have specific geographical associations is by noting which words occur most frequently alongside them. If we look at the use of words relating to migration in contemporary American English we see the following sets of associations for six of the most frequent naming choices:

BOAT PEOPLE	EMIGRANT	EXPATRIATE	IMMIGRANT	MIGRANT	REFUGEE
PEOPLE	IRISH	AMERICAN	ILLEGAL	WORKERS	CAMPS
HAITIAN	NUMBER	COMMUNITY	LEGAL	LABOR	CAMP
VIETNAMESE	LETTERS	LIVING	GROUPS	FARM	PALESTINIAN
VIETNAM	AMERICA	IRAQI	UNDOCUMENTED	WORKER	MILLION
CUBAN	TRADE	WORKERS	MEXICAN	RURAL	THOUSANDS
HAITI	GERMAN	COMMUNITIES	CHINESE	LABORERS	RETURN
EXODUS	TRANSPORTATION	BRITISH	RECENT	MEXICAN	COMMISSIONER
FLOOD	MAJORITY	ARAB	EUROPEAN	FAMILIES	STATUS
THOUSANDS	TRAIL	AMERICANS	ASIAN	ILLEGAL	NATIONS
FLED	CANADA	ENGLISH	WORKERS	URBAN	HAITIAN

As the table shows, the word "expatriate" co-occurs with "American" and "British", while "immigrant" does not. The nationalities occurring simultaneously with the word "immigrant" are "Mexican" and "Chinese". And the most frequently co-occurring word is "illegal", which also occurs with "migrant".

Naming is a choice which reflects not just a process, but a view of that process and the people involved. This becomes yet more evident when considering the terms "immigrant" and "emigrant". Which could be dismissed as simply relational antonyms, reflecting two perspectives of the same process.

However, looking at an older version of American English we see that while the use of the name "emigrant" has decreased over time, "immigrant" has increased.

Historically, "emigrants" referred to people who moved to America in the 19th and 20th Centuries from Ireland, France and England. The difference then is not due to the perspective from which the speaker regards migration, it is a difference of identity. "Immigrant" tends to refer to "others", while "emigrant" tends to refer to "us".

THE CONSEQUENCES

There are differences in the meanings of the words used to describe migration and they are largely in interpretation. But in the end, what is in a name? Does the choice of one over another make a difference? As a linguist I am bound to say yes, but in the case of migration the choices made have very real implications.

The expression of particular attitudes by powerful voices will have an effect on the attitudes of others.

So when the Australian government promotes the names "illegal arrivals" or "illegal maritime arrivals" to refer to those seeking asylum, there are consequences.

The Associated Press dropped the term "illegal immigrant" in 2013 and The Guardian has similarly questioned its use of the term.

When people are deemed "illegal" – particularly by officials – it erases our shared humanity. Things that are shared are discarded in order to highlight only differences – "they" are not like "us".

That makes the debate over the "right" term to use in relation to human migration controversial. Naming choices reflect differing attitudes and can have detrimental consequences.

1. In the mid-2010s, media organizations writing about the Syrian refugee crisis began changing the words they used to describe the people arriving in other countries from Syria, choosing words they believed would show less bias and would be more fair to the people they wrote about. Do you think word choice shows bias? What are some words media organizations use when telling stories that show a particular bias?

2. The Associated Press stopped calling some immigrants "illegal immigrants" in 2013, after deciding the term was unfair. However, many governments still refer to refugees or other migrants seeking asylum as illegal immigrants because they did not come through the proper channels for immigration. Does the unwillingness of certain media organizations to use the language of the governments show a bias toward migrants? Does it show a bias against the government?

"MEDIA BIAS AND THE 'NEWS' FORM: A HISTORICAL CRITIQUE," BY MATT BOLTON, FROM *NOVARA MEDIA*, MARCH 27, 2016

There is nothing new about the question of media bias against the left. It has been a perennial allegation from leftist activists and politicians virtually from the moment there was a media to be biased and a left to be biased against. Nonetheless, the reaction to Jeremy Corbyn's election as Labour leader has reached such deranged levels of contempt (from the liberal press as much as the right) that it has become a central political issue once again – not since the attacks on the so-called 'loony left' Labour councils of the 1980s has the partisan nature of the media been so apparent.

The puzzle is why so many journalists are oblivious to this new reality – genuinely convinced they are acting *objectively*, merely 'reporting the facts'. The easy answer would be that they are lying, or acting in bad faith. This argument underpins a common critique of the media from a leftist position, one which points to the explicit, conscious bias visible in partisan language and deliberate distortion, and usually attributes it to the hidden political affiliation of journalists. Other critiques focus instead on the implicit bias derived from the dominant class background (posh), race (white), and gender (male) of journalists. Alternatively, 'structural' analyses tend to explain bias by highlighting patterns of media ownership, arguing that the concentration of major newspapers and TV networks in the hands of a tiny number of private individuals and corporations enables them to disproportionately influence the political agenda.

Each of these critiques is crucial. But there is a further point of analysis which is invariably ignored altogether: that of the *form* of 'news' journalism itself. In a media-saturated society, the organisation of information-as-news constitutes a form which is imposed on virtually everything, whether it makes the grade as 'newsworthy' or not – an ordering of history which is so routine we barely notice it. The ubiquity of this form not only shapes our understanding of history but acts concretely upon it, in such a way that, like the police, its effects cannot be removed merely by a change of personnel or ownership. Treating the news form as essentially benign fails to recognise that news is not natural but a historical product. It did not emerge fully formed, or develop in isolation, but co-evolved historically with methods of technical production and the structures of media ownership.

I want to attempt to grasp and critique the form of 'news' on its own terms – to delineate the framework within which explicit distortion and implicit bias may, or may not, take place. In short, by accepting journalists' own premises (that they are acting in good faith, and behaving impartially) I want to show how the development of the news form has stamped the journalistic processing of the world in politically tendentious ways, long before questions of conscious bias are raised.

How, then, do news journalists perceive their own role? What do they *think* they are doing? One answer was provided by former BBC political editor Nick Robinson in an interview at the Frontline club. Asked whether his motivation as a journalist was to 'change the world', he disagreed, insisting that all he wanted to do was explain:

I get kick out of thinking 'that [subject] is incredibly complicated, can I get my head round it and explain it,' and I don't really care what you [the viewer] think at the end of it, genuinely, I couldn't care less whether you end up thinking it's good or bad, but if you come away thinking 'oh right, I get [it]'...The nicest thing anyone says to me...is 'you said that and I really understand it now.' I go home skipping when that happens.

From this perspective, journalism is the identification, clarification and re-presentation of a piece of information. This information should be explained in such a way that it stands alone as understandable in itself, minimising the need for extraneous knowledge, and is conveyed without recourse to any external moral or political judgement. But might not the work of many academic researchers be characterised in the same way? What is it that distinguishes the identification and explanation of a piece of information in general, as might take place in any field of intellectual work, from one that is 'newsworthy'? This is especially pressing given the wide range of subjects and global locations juxtaposed as 'the news' in any single paper or broadcast. What is it that holds them all together in one recognisable form, separating them from other modes of information?

The obvious answer is the one that stares back from the top of the (web)page – what Benedict Anderson describes as 'calendrical coincidence'. Each piece of information in a news bulletin or newspaper, no matter how geographically distant or unrelated in content, gained the status of a 'story' on the same date. Every day (or hour, or minute) brings with it a new round of news – different in content, yet identical in form to that of the day or hour before. It is therefore a shared temporality, a peculiar 'now-ness' of journalistic time, which unites and identifies otherwise disparate facts as 'the news'. This distinct form of temporality is founded upon the fragmentation of time into identical demarcated periods, which follow one another in an irreversible march of hours, days, months and years. These identical fragments have no necessary content. They measure nothing but time itself. The relentless progression of what Anderson calls 'empty, homogenous time' is the fundamental assumption upon which the entire edifice of the news is built.

A journalist's job depends on their ability to extract new *stories* from the daily progression of that 'empty, homogenous time'. This task entails a second fragmentation – the breaking up of regimented daily time into a series of events, each of which can be separated from the broader flux, fixed in position and presented as a singular story. The isolation of a single, static event requires the imposition of a narrative, with a clear beginning and end – 'who, what, where, when, why', as the journalists' manual has it. Once an event has been isolated, a decision must be made as to whether it makes the grade as newsworthy or not. This is essentially dependent on the measurement of change or novelty the story represents. For a particular change to be regarded as news, it must be foregrounded against a contextual background which, while it might move forward in time, is assumed to be essentially the same. The bigger the change that can be distinguished from an 'empty, homogenous' background, the more the story merits being described as 'newsworthy'. Once this title has been bestowed, a 'time-sensitive' premium is placed on any other event which can appear as a further manifestation of that change, regardless of whether it would normally merit coverage. The exceptionalism of the event is reinforced by its repetition in a cluster of near-identical stories.

There are certainly some aspects of some situations for which the narrative form of the 'event' can potentially aid understanding – establishing the details of what took place during an incident of police violence, for example. But the generalised application of this form to the whole of society necessarily leads to the prioritisation of 'changes' – which can be positively identified as such – over patterns of social relations which do not emerge as isolated incidents but have become naturalised, subsumed within the 'empty background' of everyday life. A violent murder in a rich neighbourhood is a story. The daily grind of oppressive poverty is not. Sexual assaults committed by a group of supposed migrants is a story. Run-of-the-mill sexual harassment in the office is not. The decision over what constitutes an event, and what is dissolved into the flat background, is undoubtedly a moment in the journalistic process where explicit and implicit bias can have a huge impact. But even if we grant journalists the best of intentions, it is clear that this fixation on events leads to an understanding of history which is fractured and one dimensional. For the media, history is a collection of events strung out in a line, one after another. These events are assiduously archived and available for reference, but are not understood as having any essential connection. History itself has no movement, aside from the ticking of homogenous empty time.

Here it becomes clear why a news story cannot make the grade unless it can be understood on its own terms. The isolation of a news story from its broader historical context is not a result of flawed journalistic performance. If history is essentially empty, it has no resources to offer news journalists when it comes to explaining the 'change' expressed in 'the news'. They must instead rely on identifying the supposed causes of the selected events from the inside. It is thus fundamental to the very existence of 'news', as a form in which a moment of change is thrown into relief against a one-dimensional background, that the 'event' itself be represented as the driver of its own movement. It must become self-evident.

CAPITALIST TIME, CAPITALIST FREEDOM

The origins of journalism's fragmented temporality can be found in the traditional periodic pattern of media publication – the morning or evening newspaper, the daily TV or radio news broadcast. It is no coincidence this regular schedule matches that of the 'industrial time' of capitalist production, in which social life is split into a repetitive series of 'work days', each ruled by the merciless ticking of the clock. From the outset, the newspaper was an institution explicitly set to the rhythms of commercial capitalism. In *The Long Revolution* Raymond Williams writes: "[t]he newspaper was the creation of the commercial middle class, mainly in the eighteenth century. It served this class with news relevant to the conduct of business." Early content was dedicated solely to the current state of markets, shipping, stock prices, exports and imports.

Although initially barred from reporting on parliamentary proceedings, the increasing 'freedom of the press' went hand-in-hand with the gradual political domination by the commercial class whom that press served. This 'freedom' was underpinned by the rise of advertising as an independent financial basis for expanding circulation, which encouraged the replacement of direct state control of printing presses by a stamp tax. Press freedom can therefore be regarded as the flipside of a process by which news no longer merely focused on the movement of commodities but became a full commodity itself – and as such was predicated on the acceptance of a society ruled by the commercial class. Any direct challenge to this state of affairs, and the 'freedom' of the press would soon run into limits.

This was made starkly apparent by the treatment of alternative forms of printed communication that had developed in the shadow of the bourgeois press. Radical periodicals such as William Cobbett's *Political Register* or Thomas Wooler's *Black Dwarf* faced fierce political repression as demands for parliamentary reform reached a head in the early 19th century, as well as severe financial constraints. They were able to survive and find a large audience in the atmosphere of political turmoil running up to the 1832 Reform Act – in part by shifting from news to political opinion, in an attempt to avoid stamp taxes. But as resistance faded in the Act's aftermath, the commercial and political advantages held by the bourgeois press eventually meant it was able to overwhelm all other modes of communication, subsuming them within its own market-determined form.

The radical press never died out entirely, as the later success of the Chartist press attests, but it struggled to compete on a mass level with the commercial media once the advertising model of funding took hold. Publishers who could not match the higher levels of investment folded, and the number of newspaper titles in print contracted. But the circulation of those that remained expanded enormously, thanks in part to advertisement-funded investment in new printing techniques, which cheapened costs and reduced prices. The extension of such a model of journalism to a mass audience was therefore based on that audience's integration into the market as consumers. As Williams argues:

> The fact is the economic organisation of the press in Britain has been predominantly in terms of the commercial middle class which the newspapers first served. When papers organised in this way [they] reached out to a wider public, they brought in the new readers on a market basis and not by means of participation or genuine community relationships...The community as a whole was not providing its newspapers, but having them provided for it by particular interests.

From the outset, then, journalists worked under the assumption that their readers were the individual consumers of a capitalist society. Any collective identity that a media outlet might try to build from its readership (the 'we' evoked in countless Sunday supplement articles) is necessarily founded upon that of the isolated consumer. Mediatised collective subjectivity cannot contribute to the destruction of the market individual, because it is entirely predicated upon that individual. It thus ends up being reduced to an expression of shared consumption preferences (including political 'persuasion'), or a form of nationalist 'belonging'. Forms of collective experience which do not fit into the straitjacket of consumer preference cannot be accounted for. Through the eyes of a media grounded in advertising and individual consumption, they simply do not exist.

OBJECTIVITY AND ITS PRESUPPOSITIONS

Like all capitalist enterprises, the media relies on the continual emergence of new commodities ('stories') from the daily cycle of production. The demands of profit made it imperative to minimise the time between the moment of journalistic production and that of consumption, placing speed and 'topicality' at the centre of journalistic practice. Investment in new technology, in part driven by competition between rival papers, has continually shortened the temporal lag between the journalistic processing of the 'event' and its consumption by the reader. Today, this gap has almost been closed entirely, undermining the traditional periodic structure of the daily newspaper in the process.

The key technological development which set the 'time-space compression' of news in motion was the invention of the telegraph. The ability to send a telegram allowed journalists to file reports from distant locations without first having to travel back to the office. This new reliance on technology did not merely speed up the transmission of a news form that remained essentially the same — its impact was felt on the form itself. Before the use of the telegram, Williams argues, the style of writing in newspapers was similar to that of books – expansive, circuitous, if not verbose. Once the use of the telegraph was established, "[t]he desire for compression, to save money on the wire, led to shorter sentences and a greater emphasis of key-words. There is often a gain in simplicity and a lack of padding; often a loss in the simplification of complicated issues, and in the distorting tendency of the key-word."

'Keyword' is a crucial term for Williams – words which are the sites of battles over meaning, and which act as "ways not only of discussing but of seeing many of our central experiences." The new financially-driven emphasis on brevity meant that more weight was put onto certain terms which now carried a much greater burden of assumed knowledge and presumed shared under-standing. Journalism was no longer a medium in which the contested meanings of words could be explored, but rather one in which language was reduced to one dimen-sion by the twin demands of speed and cost. This has had lasting effects, despite the costs of communication drop-ping exponentially – the widespread use of deeply ideo-logical terms today as shorthand ('housing ladder', 'riot', 'moderate', 'credible') testifies to the hidden assumptions built into the formal conventions of journalistic language.

The processes by which the backdrop of news came to be regarded as essentially unchanging, and the language of journalism boiled down to a skeleton of presuppositions, developed in relation to that of the much vaunted (and criticised) 'objectivity' of the news form. It was no accident that the new 'objective' style of journalism emerged in the aftermath of the defeat of the Chartist movement in the 1850s, a period in which class struggle temporarily retreated. The mid-19th century, writes Williams, "saw the consolidation of sentiment from the middle class upwards," meaning that "most newspapers were able to drop their frantic pamphleteering, and to serve this public with news and a regulated diversity of opinion."

There is no doubt that the new focus on the straight reporting of 'facts' was an improvement on the previous forms of 'faction' which littered the early newspapers. But this supposedly new and more objective journalism was ultimately predicated upon an assumption that political conflict was now settled: the inherent contradictions of class society were erased from view. Disagreement might continue to exist, but was now reduced to questions of technical management of a society in which everyone was heading in the same direction, and where the fundamental relations were fixed in place.

Journalistic objectivity, and the all-encompassing expansion of a commodified media model, should therefore be regarded as historically specific products of a period of capitalist entrenchment. Both were expressions of a presumed agreement about the shape and direction of a rational and 'well-ordered' society – in other words, the naturalisation of capitalist social relations. To this end, the 'apolitical' objectivity of the news story, and the flattening of meaning in journalistic language, correlates to the reified form of the market in classical political economy. Here, the market appears as an isolated *economic* sphere, separated from politics and governed by its own objective laws which, if left alone, will work for the good of the whole. If things seem to be getting worse, rather than better (the underlying message of every story in papers like the *Daily Mail*, *Express* or *Telegraph*), the blame must be placed on untoward intervention in that supposedly objective sphere – via conspiracy, the 'nanny state', or 'bad apples' – rather than recognised as its inherently destructive results. It was for this reason that Georg Lukács argued the figure of the 'objective' journalist represented reification at its most grotesque: "[t]he journalist's 'lack of convictions', the prostitution of his experiences and beliefs is comprehensible only as the apogee of capitalist reification."

It is thus this hypostatisation of social relations, the presupposition that political conflict has been resolved and contradiction removed from society, which constitutes the 'flat background' from which the news is 'objectively' drawn. This demand for inherent explanation means news stories invariably end up flattening complex historical processes in order to pinpoint the individual actions (who, what, where, when, why) which appear to have directly produced the phenomenon under scrutiny. When it comes to assigning motivation for actions, the habitual practices of 'objective' journalism – founded upon the denial of any legitimate reasons for conflict and resistance – are reinforced by the use of a language in which meaning has been frozen. This leaves few options available for a plausible inherent explanation, aside from 'irrationality', 'madness' or 'evil'. Such 'self-evident' explanations inevitably lead to the scapegoating of those deemed personally responsible for the evil actions, and the incessant demand that 'something must be done' to eradicate their nefarious influence. It is this dynamic which underlies the recurrent characterisation of leftist movements and political leaders as 'mad' or 'loony'. If political struggle is settled, and contradiction expelled, any opposition to 'society as it is' cannot be regarded as rational. From the perspective of 'the news' it is, rather, genuinely inexplicable.

Paradoxically, it is this same dynamic which is utilised by the media when faced with the substantive historical change its very existence as 'news' denies. From Hillsborough to anti-racism, the news form is able to recuperate the results of long, hard-fought struggles – struggles usually opposed by the media at the time – only by pushing legitimate conflict backwards, safely into the past. The mantra of 'of course, it was different back then' grants approval to certain historic conflicts (namely, those whose effects have been so powerful they cannot be ignored), not by recognising inherent contradiction but by inverting the relation of rationality. Society itself is, when necessary, scapegoated in retrospect ('back then') as an unfortunate but necessary stepping stone in the gradual progression of things, while once-demonised protesters are transformed into the pioneering bearers of a rationality which has thankfully been realised in 'society as it is' today.

The effect of this is to drain past struggles of any contemporary relevance. The possibility that the same contradictory pressures which fed into historic conflict might do the same today is not only denied, but done so in the name of the 'rational' protesters of the past. Thus those involved in the 2011 English riots were depicted in the media as 'mindless' in comparison to the rioters of 1981, who were retrospectively reassessed and deemed to have had genuine cause to protest – despite the media at the time characterising those riots in precisely the same 'mindless' fashion. In this way the results of past struggles are naturalised, dissolved into the 'flat background' of the news, and thereby used to reinforce the supposed inevitability of the current state of society. This ensures opposition to today's society can continue to be treated as 'irrational'.

THE BATTLE OF THE SCAPEGOAT

In historical periods where people were able to develop political knowledge through non-mediatised collective institutions (political parties, trade unions, religious bodies), the peculiar presuppositions of the news form were not yet those of society as a whole. But as those alternative means of political education have all but collapsed, the media has expanded to fill the gap. This has left the political process itself at the mercy of the insatiable temporal and explanatory demands of the news.

One way in which these demands become manifest is through the proliferation of the journalistic deadline, the limit point that splits time into a 'before' and 'after'. The media's constant need for new events that fit into the framework of abstract time has shifted the 'deadline' from a technique internal to the production schedule of the newspaper office to a temporal framework which can be used to apply the form of the event onto almost anything. The imposition of deadlines enables, say, the sort of polit-ical negotiations normally regarded as dull, drawn-out affairs to be transformed into tension-filled events by their presentation as 'races against time' for deals to be struck. The strident demand that 'something must be done' before 'time runs out' has severe material consequences for both the process and results of those negotiations.

Similarly, the way in which economic data is chopped up into media-friendly temporal fragments allows the form of the event to be imposed upon the slow, contradictory unfolding of economic 'development'. This then feeds into the spectacle of media-led celebration at the 'recovery event' signalled by +0.2% growth in one 'quarter', and deep despair at the 'recession event' demonstrated by -0.2% the next. In both cases, the *longue durée* of political and economic processes – in other words, history itself – is erased by the self-contained immediacy of the reportable event, forced into existence by the striation of the deadline.

The forward drive implied by the ticking of 'homogenous, empty time' constantly pushes news stories to fixate on the future, on what will happen 'next'. This enables the media to construct longer narrative arcs, which give both impetus and a sense of self-fulfilling inevitability to the personalised explanation of the news. History is erased by a projected future, one which derives from the assumption of a one-dimensional society in which conflict is resolved. Once a politician is trapped within such an arc, it is almost impossible to escape, for good or for ill. Compare the relative positions of Jeremy Corbyn and Boris Johnson. As a critic of 'society as it is', Corbyn has found himself caught within a narrative arc in which he is congenitally irrational, 'mad', and dangerous – destined for embarrassing and deeply damaging failure. There is literally nothing he can do which will not be criticised on these terms. Johnson, meanwhile, is in the opposite position, the protagonist of a narrative in which he is beloved by all who cross his path, and is destined for a glorious ascension to Number 10. The abject failures of his period as Mayor of London have no bearing whatsoever on the progression of this arc, to the extent that they have not merited more than a handful of critical questions from journalists throughout his entire eight year term.

The ability to manipulate such narrative arcs and arbitrary deadlines through the provision of personalised explanation and clearly identifiable scapegoats has therefore become one of the key criteria by which to judge the 'success' of a politician. An entire industry of commentators and analysts – those inducted into the 'cult of savvy', as media theorist Jay Rosen describes those who purport to 'know how the game works' – exists solely to weigh up the respective merits of political actors in this regard. The pervasive effect of the need to fulfil such demands has now spread across the whole of political discourse, and can be seen particularly clearly with regard to the financial crash of 2008 and its after-math. While the right pin the blame for the crash on the Labour government's 'overspending' on public services, the anti-austerity left have instead attempted to shift the focus onto the actions of 'the bankers' or 'the 1%'. The names of the scapegoats may change, but both positions are ultimately founded on the assumption that if only those individual 'causes' could be eradicated, the economy would return to a kind of natural equilibrium. A deeper understanding of the inherent relation of crisis to capi-talism – a relation which can be only be seen historically – is therefore obfuscated by the temporal requirements of the news form. Politics becomes a battle of ensuring one scapegoat receives more blame than the other.

This poses no real problems for the right – theirs is a worldview in which the market, kept free of all untoward intervention, really does provide the best of all possible worlds. This assumption lies at the root of the Conservative government's narrative over both the cause of the crash and the solution – that public spending cuts will lead to the 'elimination of the deficit' by a certain date. The reason why these arguments have been so convincing to so many (with journalists at the forefront) has very little to do with their veracity. Rather, their success is based upon the skilful way in which the 'story' of both the causes of the crash and its austerity solution have been shaped to fit into the media-friendly form of the event, with its demand for inherent, personalised explanations and clear narrative arcs. The same dynamic is at work when media-savvy politicians rage against any suggestion historical context might shed some light on acts of terrorism, and insist banally that 'the terrorists are solely responsible for their actions'. It is simply not possible for a left founded on an understanding of the inherent instability of capitalist society – expressed by contradictions which emerge, in Karl Marx's words, as part of "a social process that goes on behind the backs" of individuals – to win on these terms. To attempt to do so is to relinquish any claim to history as something more than a collection of contingent events, and to fade into a sanitised shadow of the right.

There are no easy solutions to this problem. The replacement of corporate media monopolies by democratically-controlled organisations is no small demand. Nor is ending the domination of journalism by privately-educated white men. Both would go a long way to eradicating much explicit and implicit media bias, particularly when it comes to the process by which events are selected as 'newsworthy'. But neither of these measures on its own challenges the hegemony of the news as form. The dominance of this form is such that even non-commodified media organisations such as the BBC are completely under its sway. In any case, the BBC was never intended to challenge the *form* of news, but merely the private ownership of its means of production and distribution. And even while the advertising funding model of the press collapses, the form persists, and gathers strength. Social media does potentially provide a real alternative, but it too has by no means escaped the power of 'the news'.

From one angle, it offers the tools by which the presuppositions of the news might be dismantled, raising the possibility that the self-evident explanations, fragmented temporality and hypostatised language of the media might be broken down and given new historical meaning. From another, it merely speeds up the process of the branding and circulation of 'events' and scapegoats integral to the news. The news form is not something which merely exists on the page, and which can be simply circumnavigated by peer-to-peer communication networks. It shapes the actual world around us, the way we experience our own lives and understand our history. We live through the news form, and it will not give up its hold without a fight.

1. The media is a business, as the author points out, and it is a journalist's job to write or report new stories every day. Because journalists are required

to produce so much content, do you think there's more of a chance for media bias now than there would be if we didn't have 24/7 news? Or does the immense amount of media available mean there's less chance of bias? Explain.

2. The author discusses ways in which the public learned information when there were fewer media outlets, such as from labor unions, political parties, and places of worship. What are ways you can get information now without relying on corporate or government-run media outlets? Are these sources of information likely to me more or less biased than the media? Why do you think this?

"NAVIGATING WAR: HAS THE WAR IN SYRIA ALSO DESTROYED JOURNALISM?" BY RAMZY BAROUD, FROM *COMMON DREAMS*, DECEMBER 15, 2016

When a veteran war reporter like Robert Fisk constructs his argument regarding the siege of Aleppo based on 'watching' video footage, then one can truly comprehend the near impossibility of adequate media coverage on the war in Syria.

In a recent article in the British *Independent*, Fisk reflects on the siege, uprising and atrocious Nazi massacres in Warsaw, Poland in 1944. The terribly high cost of that war leads him to reject the French assertion that the current siege in Aleppo is the 'worst massacre since World War Two.'

"Why do we not see the defending fighters, as we do on the Warsaw films? Why are we not told about their political allegiance, as we most assuredly are on the Warsaw footage? Why do we not see 'rebel' military hardware—as well as civilian targets—being hit by artillery and air attack as we do on the Polish newsreels?," he asks, further demonstrating what he perceives to be the flaw of such a comparison.

Not that Fisk doubts that pictures of the dead and wounded children in eastern Aleppo are real; his argument is largely against the one-sidedness of the coverage, of demonizing one party, while sparing another.

Without reserve, I always find comparing massacres—to find out which is worse—tasteless, if not inhumane. What is the point in this, aside from mitigating the effect of a terrible tragedy, by comparing it to a hypothetically much greater tragedy? Or, as the French have done, perhaps exaggerating the human toll to create the type of fear that often leads to reckless political and military action?

The French and other NATO countries have used this tactic repeatedly in the past. In fact, this is how the war on Libya was concocted, purportedly to stave off the imminent Tripoli 'genocide' and Benghazi 'bloodbath.' The Americans used it in Iraq, successfully. The Israelis have perfected it in Gaza.

In fact, the United States' intervention in Iraq was always tied to some sort of imagined global threat that, unsurprisingly, was never proven. Former British Prime Minister, Tony Blair, was so eager to take part in the conquest of Iraq in 2003 that he contrived intelligence alleging that Iraq, under Saddam Hussein, was able to deploy weapons of mass destruction within 45 minutes from the moment such an order was given.

The US went even further: it was only recently revealed that the US had hired a London-based firm, Bell Pottinger, to create fake al-Qaeda videos and news reports that were designed to appear as if written by legitimate Arabic media.

The propaganda videos were 'personally approved' by the commander of the US-led coalition forces in Iraq at the time, General David Petraeus, Salon and others reported.

We still do not know the specific content of many of these videos and to what extent such material, which cost US tax payers $540 million dollars, influenced events on the ground and our understanding of these events.

Considering the high financial cost and the fact that the company worked directly from inside Baghdad's 'Camp Victory', 'side-by-side' with high-ranking US officials, one can only imagine the degree of deceit imparted upon innocent viewers and readers for years.

Compounded with the fact that the whole reason behind the war was a lie, the then Secretary of Defense, Donald Rumsfeld, had no intention of ever informing reporters of what was really transpiring on the ground, and that countless reporters agreed to be 'embedded' with US-British forces, thus further contributing to the one-sided narrative. One is left to wonder if any truth ever emerged from Iraq.

Then, again, we know that hundreds of thousands have died in that catastrophic military adventure, that Iraq is not better off, and that thousands more are still being killed because this is what happens when countries are invaded, destabilized, hurriedly reassembled and then left to lick their wounds, alone.

The chaotic violence and sectarianism in Iraq are the direct outcome of the US invasion and occupation, which were constructed on official lies and dishonest media reporting.

Is it too much to ask, then, that we learn from those dreadful mistakes, to understand that when all is said and done, nothing will remain but mass graves and grieving nations?

As for the lies that enable wars, and allow the various sides to clinch on their straw arguments of selected morality, few ever have the intellectual courage to take responsibility when they are proven wrong. We simply move on, uncaring for the victims of our intellectual squabbles.

"The extreme bias shown in foreign media coverage of similar events in Iraq and Syria will be a rewarding subject for PhD students looking at the uses and abuses of propaganda down the ages," wrote war reporter, Patrick Cockburn.

He is right, of course, but as soon as his report on media bias was published, he was attacked and dismissed by both sides on social media. From their perspective, a proper position would be for him to completely adopt the version of events as seen by one side, and totally ignore the other.

Yet, with both sides of the war having no respect for media or journalists—the list of journalists killed in Syria keeps on growing—no impartial journalist is allowed to carry out his or her work in accordance with the minimum standards of reporting.

Thus, the 'truth' can only be gleaned based on deductive reasoning—as many of us have successfully done, reporting on Iraq and Palestine.

Of course, there will always been the self-tailored activist-journalist-propagandist variety who will continue to cheer for death and destruction in the name of whatever ideology they choose to follow. They abide by no reasoning, but their own convenient logic – that which is only capable of demonizing their enemies and lionizing their friends.

Unfortunately, these media trolls are the ones shaping the debate on much of what is happening in the Middle East today.

While the coverage of war in the past has given rise to many daring journalists—Seymour Hersh in Vietnam, Tariq Ayyoub in Iraq, photo-journalist Zoriah Miller, and hundreds more—the war in Syria is destroying journalistic integrity and, with it, our readers' ability to decipher one of the most convoluted conflicts of the modern era.

In Syria, as in Iraq and other warring regions in the Middle East, the 'truth' is not shaped by facts, but opinions, themselves fashioned by blind allegiances, not truly humanistic principles or even simple common sense.

"Loyalty to petrified opinions never yet broke a chain or freed a human soul in this world—and never will," wrote Mark Twain many years ago.

It was true then, as it is true in the Middle East today.

1. The author suggests that war reporting is inherently biased because of the conditions journalists must work under and how they have to operate in order to protect their access to the situation as well as to protect themselves. Do you think that covering a war is likely to lead to more bias than other types of news reporting? Should journalists covering a war be held to different standards?

2. In most wars, there is a "good" side and a "bad" side — the Nazis versus the Allies in World War II, or the US versus al-Qaeda during the Iraq War. Should journalists be required to give both sides of a war equal deference? Or is it permissible for journalists to be biased in certain instances? What would those instances be?

"IN BRAZIL, JOURNALISTS FACE INJURY FROM VIOLENT PROTESTS AND ACCUSATIONS OF BIAS," BY ANDREW DOWNIE, FROM THE COMMITTEE TO PROTECT JOURNALISTS, SEPTEMBER 20, 2016

Felipe Souza was covering an anti-government protest in São Paulo earlier this month when a line of riot police advanced toward him.

Souza was facing the officers and wearing a helmet, a gas mask (to protect him from tear gas) and a bullet-proof vest that identified him as a reporter for BBC Brasil. As the troops got closer, he stood with his back to a wall and raised his hands to show he was unarmed and unthreatening.

The gesture was futile.

"'Get out of the way! Move! Move!' at least four officers said before hitting me with their batons on my right forearm, my left hand, my right shoulder, my chest, and my right leg," Souza recounted in a piece for the BBC Brasil website. "One of them called me garbage."

Souza escaped without serious injury but the incident is indicative of the increasing dangers faced by journalists covering Brazil's tumultuous political and social movements.

The country has faced turmoil since 2013, when millions took to the streets to protest issues including rising bus fares, extravagant spending on World Cup stadiums, and a lack of investment in health, education, and social services.

In August President Dilma Rousseff, who was elected for a first term in 2010 and re-elected four years later, was removed from office after a drawn-out impeachment process that many criticized as illegitimate.

Protesters both for and against her impeachment have taken to the streets to show their support or opposition and journalists--particularly at demonstrations in support of her presidency and against her successor Michel Temer--have come under fire on a regular basis.

Since those first demonstrations in May 2013, at least 293 journalists, bloggers, and photographers have been victims of aggression while covering street protests, according to the Brazilian Association of Investigative Journalism (ABRAJI).

The attacks documented by the association include cases of reporters being on the receiving end of tear gas and rubber bullets, being beaten in truncheon attacks, and harassed by protesters. In some cases, the police seized equipment and erased information on cell phones or cameras.

Almost half of the incidents took place in Brazil's biggest city São Paulo and "more than half of those (62%) were deliberate," the Brazilian Association of Investigative Journalism said. "In other words, the professional had identified him or herself as a journalist at work. Nevertheless, they were still detained or victimized." The police were responsible for 71 percent of the incidents but many also came from demonstrators angry at perceived press bias, and there has been a worrying uptick in attacks carried out by protesters.

Between January and September this year, demonstrators were responsible for 40 percent of all attacks against the press, according to the ombudsman at the *Folha de S.Paulo*, a newspaper whose main head-quarters has come under attack from protesters.

Police said they were responding to vandals, according to reports.

Folha's newsroom editor did not respond to repeated requests for an interview and neither did officials with TV Globo, the television arm of Brazil's biggest media empire whose reporters are often targeted because of its perceived anti-Workers' Party stance.

However, editors at other publications said they have had to rethink how to deploy their reporters.

"We have difficulties covering the protests," said Diego Escosteguy, the unabashedly anti-Rousseff editor-in-chief of weekly newsmagazine *Época*. "Our first concern is the safety of the reporters and when there is a protest there is a debate about how to get our reporters to them safely. I can't go. I've had concrete threats that if I go to a demonstration against Temer or for Dilma then I'll get beaten up. I would like to hear people but I can't, and that's a sign of how toxic things have become." He added that he had received threatening calls, as well as threatening messages on social media.

The physical dangers--organizations including the BBC and Reuters put all their reporters through hostile environment training--have been accompanied by a sharpening of discourse at both ends of the political spectrum. Public attitudes hardened in the lead up to

Rousseff's ouster and journalists say their reporting is coming under the microscope.

"I have worked in a lot of countries that are extremely polarized or where people have extreme opinions--including Israel, Haiti, Cuba, Venezuela, Mexico--and it has taken me by surprise here because Brazil doesn't have a history of this kind of political tension," NPR reporter Lourdes Garcia-Navarro told CPJ over the phone from her home in Rio de Janeiro. "There is a concerted campaign from people both inside and outside the media to give this a narrative, their narrative."

The situation is harder for local reporters who face pressure not just from editors and readers but also from friends and family. Amplified on social media, the scrutiny has gone way beyond the normal, long-respected boundaries.

"We are always being accused of being for the left or for the right or of hiding something," Caio Quero, the executive editor of BBC Brasil, told CPJ. "It is daily occurrence and it's such that even things that have nothing to do with politics, people are now relating them to politics. If we write about women's rights or indigenous rights or racism we are called communists. And if we write about pension or labor reform or budget cuts we are accused of being capitalists or agents of British imperialism."

The media have also been accused of fomenting the divide.

Popular news magazines such as *Veja* and *Isto É* came out in favor of impeachment but most publications have been less partisan. The situation was summarized by Glenn Greenwald, the Rio-based journalist and co-founder of *The Intercept*, who tweeted that there was a reason to denounce "Brazil's oligarch-owned media as [a] threat to free press."

In an email response to CPJ's questions, Greenwald, who recently announced the launch of a Brazilian edition of *The Intercept*, said, "Impeachment was a complex question with nuanced considerations, but the Brazilian media alternated between covering it as a Manichean drama and agitating for it to happen." Greenwald added, "They thus played a large role in this hardening and polarization."

It would be hard to predict what will happen next in Brazil but there is a sense that while the institutional upheaval is complete, respite for the media may be fleeting. Protests against Temer are likely to continue and last week's indictment of former President Luiz Inácio Lula da Silva on corruption charges has inflamed passions further.

"I think that it will calm down a bit in the next few months but proposed reforms are not popular and when they are on the table I think we will see a reaction from the unions and social movements," said the BBC's Quero. "I think we are the end of one process and the start of another."

1. In Brazil, journalists have been deliberately attacked by people who believe the journalists' outlets are especially biased against the

attackers' side. Many journalists have also been detained by the police while covering demonstrations. Can you imagine this happening in the US? Discuss instances when American journalists have faced similar hazards doing their jobs in their home country.

2. Brazilian media outlets showed a bias through their editorializing and calling for impeachment of the country's president. But media outlets have always had news and opinion sections. Do you think an outlet's editorial opinion should be held against it as a bias even if its news reporting seems fair? What would you do to make sure an outlet's editorial and opinion pieces don't influence the news?

CHAPTER 6

WHAT ORDINARY PEOPLE SAY

Everyone has an opinion about the media,-because everyone consumes some form of news. Whether you get your news from Facebook and Twitter, from CNN and Fox News, from C-SPAN, from the *New York Times* or the *Wall Street Journal*, from Vox and the Verge or the Daily Beast, you're participating in the media and choosing a perspective and angle you prefer when receiving information. And chances are, you have reasons for choosing the outlets you do and for your beliefs about the outlets you choose to avoid — and so do your friends and neighbors. In this chapter, you'll read what other everyday people think about the news and media bias. From bloggers and online columnists to everyday people interviewed on the street, you'll explore what the public thinks about the media and why they view it the way they do—from people questioning which came first, the media bias or the polarized political environment, to bloggers questioning the decisions their preferred news outlets make, to student journalists who wonder what the media landscape would look like if there wasn't media bias.

"MAINSTREAM MEDIA BIAS: AL JAZEERA BLOCKS ARTICLE CRITICIZING SAUDI ARABIA FOR HUMAN RIGHTS VIOLATIONS," BY AMANDO FLAVIO, FROM ANONHQ.COM, DECEMBER 27, 2015

When we talk of Mainstream Media bias, we are not joking. It is real. It is happening. Some of their news contents are filled with government and corporate propaganda.

What is even worse is that when there is a news item that does not favor their cronies, they try to censor it, putting their audience in the dark.

And one big Mainstream Media in the Arab World, Al Jazeera has just been exposed for blocking an article criticizing one of its closest allies, Saudi Arabia.

Al Jazeera is a State-funded broadcaster owned by the Al Jazeera Media Network, which is partly funded by the House of Thani, the ruling family of Qatar. The House of Thani is a very close ally of the House of Saud, the ruling family of Saudi Arabia.

Recently, reports emerged that Saudi Arabia was planning to execute more than 50 people in just a single day for alleged terrorist crimes. The issue sparked an outrage, with human rights campaigners actively criticizing, and petitioning World Leaders to put pressure on Saudi Arabia to stop the execution.

Although Saudi Arabia is yet to carry out the execution, rights groups are worried because this year alone, the Kingdom has executed some 151 people. This is far above the 90 people executed in 2014.

The media which broke the story that the Kingdom was preparing to execute 50 in just a single day, Okaz is said to have close ties to the Saudi Ministry of Interior, and would not have published the story without obtaining the government's consent.

It is against this background that the adjunct professor of law at the Georgetown University Law Center, Arjun Sethi took to the keyboard to express his dissatisfaction of the appalling human rights record of Saudi Arabia, and the shocking silence of World Powers, especially the United States.

Professor Sethi titled is article, "Saudi Arabia Uses Terrorism As An Excuse for Human Rights Abuses". He succeeded in getting the piece published on Al Jazeera America. Professor Sethi in the past has written several articles for Al Jazeera America and Al Jazeera English.

And according to the *Intercept*, some few days after the article was published, the corporate headquarters of Al Jazeera blocked the critical article from audience outside the United States. Al Jazeera America is owned by the Al Jazeera Media Network. It was launched in 2013 to directly compete with CNN, HLN, MSNBC, Fox News Channel, and RT America.

The *Intercepts* reports that an anonymous source in Al Jazeera America told local press that the network did not want to offend Saudi Arabia or any other State ally. The article is still available in the United States, but people attempting to view the link in other countries are given an error or "page not found".

When asked by the *Intercept* about the article, and why it was blocked, Al Jazeera's headquarters in Qatar said in a statement, "*After hearing from users from different locations across the world that several of our web pages were unavailable, we have begun investigating what the source of the problem may be and we hope to have it resolved shortly.*"

However, the Okaz newspaper later quoted a director of Al Jazeera apologizing for the article and saying that it would be removed. Another news story from a Bahraini website, showed a tweet from Al Jazeera America's account with the article's headline. For whatever reason, the tweet was later deleted. A spokesperson for Al Jazeera America would not comment on the tweet or on the discrepancy between the parent company's statement to *The Intercept* and the comments in *Okaz*.

Professor Sethi confirmed that he has come under intense personal attack from pro-Saudi accounts on Twitter. However, he said that will not deter him from speaking the truth, and seeking justice for the oppressed.

"*The trolling seemed like an organized concerted effort to intimidate me. I will not submit to this act of censorship. Human rights are universal and I will continue to litigate and write about violations wherever they occur*", he said.

1. According to the author, Al Jazeera pulled an article that was critical of the government of Saudi Arabia because it did not want to upset or offend the government. If this is true, do you think the network can be trusted to offer unbiased reporting in other instances?

2. What are steps Al Jazeera could have taken before pulling Professor Sethi's article? How would you have handled the situation?

"POLITICAL BIAS AND PERCEPTION," BY RADICAL CENTRIST, FROM THOUGHTUNDERMINED.COM, NOVEMBER 12, 2010

We all know (I hope) that our political biases colour how we view things. For example, someone with very conservative, right-wing views reading a newspaper such as The Toronto Star or The Guardian will not see their own views reflected in the editorials and commentaries (and probably not even in the way the news is reported), and so will tag those papers as being "liberal", "left-wing", etc. Ditto for someone more to the left who reads The National Post or the Daily Telegraph – they will call the paper right-wing. What is interesting to me is how media that tries to be as balanced as is humanly possible is perceived. Case in point, the Globe and Mail. If you read through reader comments, painful an exercise as that often is, you will see left-leaning people calling the Globe right-wing, while those with more conservative/right-wing views will accuse it of being part of that grand "left-wing/liberal" mainstream media conspiracy. I can only conclude then that the Globe must be succeeding in trying to be balanced, since those on each end of the political spectrum perceive it so differently. This applies to certain reporters as well. The Globe's Jane Taber is an interesting example. Comments on her "Ottawa Notebook" contributions will alternate between calling her a stooge for the Liberal Party and being a cheerleader for the current Conservative Government.

Since May, as I've immersed myself in regularly reading the British media online, I've frequently found myself quite amused at how the various sides perceive the other. Since I am not British and do not have any personal, vested interest in any of the political parties, I read a variety of sources. My daily fixtures are (in no particular order): the BBC, The Guardian, The Independent, The Daily Telegraph, ConservativeHome, New Statesman and The Spectator (mostly the blogs on those last two sites). I will occasionally read something from the more tabloidy papers, but only via a link to a story posted on something from one of the above sources.

For the unfamiliar, the above can be crudely classified this way:

Leftish and/or pro-Labour: The Guardian, New Statesman

Right-leaning and/or pro-Conservative: Daily Telegraph, ConservativeHome (obviously), The Spectator

Non-partisan: BBC, The Independent

What I find amusing is that readers of the Guardian and New Stateman will predictably lambaste any and all policies of the Coalition Government, and will be especially harsh on the Liberal Democrats and in particular Nick Clegg for supporting the Tories. There are regular comments about how it's purely a Conservative government fulfilling the Conservative Party's manifesto, that Nick Clegg is a closet (or not so closet) Tory, etc. However, if you toddle over to ConservativeHome and read the comments on the various blog posts there, you will regularly find Tories bemoaning how the Lib Dems have far too much influence in the government, how David Cameron isn't a Tory at all, but rather a closet Lib Dem (well, at least a Lib, maybe not so much a Dem), how all the true Conservative values and, more importantly, manifesto pledges, have been tossed out the window, etc. These same sorts of views can be found over on the Telegraph's site as well.

Readers of The Independent and, interestingly, the Spectator (I'm referencing the blog articles on the Spectator site) seem to be a bit more nuanced, or, shall we say, realistic?

I think, often, people aren't fully aware of their own political bias. Several years ago, when I regularly posted on a forum dedicated to Canadian politics, there was one member who was very right-wing and conservative in her views, but yet repeatedly rejected being labelled that way, claiming over and over that she was actually quite centrist. Over time I realised that she maybe thought her views were quite centrist because she mostly watched the US Fox News cable channel, and more frequently posted on US political forums that were dominated by right-wing posters. And since she probably agreed with their views, and surrounded herself with that sort of echo chamber, she saw that as being the more common, mainstream position – and anything actually more to the centre inevitably would be "left-wing".

I think regularly reading a variety of media (and the comments of readers when available), actually helps me gain a clearer sense of things. If you weed out the extremes, reality must lie somewhere in the middle. I will admit that I find it much easier to do so when it comes to British politics. I have a far more difficult time reading strongly ideological media when it comes to Canadian politics. I should rephrase that – I can read columns that take an ideological position different from mine, but I have a hard time wading through reader comments – probably because it pains me to see so many people strongly agreeing with views that don't sit well with my own. But at least I admit my own biases exist. This is much less of an issue for me when it comes to UK politics, because, as I've said, there isn't the same level of personal investment/importance, because none of the government's decisions impact me.

That said, I am noticing that I seem to be wavering on this front somewhat. I'm finding it increasingly difficult to read comments in the Guardian and New Statesman, for example, because so many of them seem to be to be gross knee-jerk reactions, particularly against the Lib Dems and Nick Clegg. A lot of the comments at ConservativeHome actually scare me because the posters are so right-wing and conservative, but these are still easier for me to read because their attacks are usually aimed at the Conservative Party leadership for not being Tory-enough. They rarely aim any criticism at the Lib Dems, accepting the coalition as a necessary inconvenience.

I frequently find myself wanting to post on the Guardian comments a suggestion that people read comments on ConservativeHome and vice versa. I still think it's largely beneficial to expose oneself to as many viewpoints as possible, even if some of them make your blood boil.

1. The author discusses ways in which they try to avoid being victim to media bias, such as by reading multiple opposing sources. What are some opposing news sources in America? How common is it, do you think, for a news source to have an opposite?

2. The author suggests that you can use oppositional news sources to get closer to the truth by comparing what each says and finding a middle ground. If you don't know a source's political bias, how can you determine a story's accuracy? What are some steps you can take, as a reader or viewer, to verify that the news you're consuming is accurate?

"ELECTION COVERAGE REFLECTS FRACTURED MEDIA LANDSCAPE, EXPERTS SAY," BY CLAIRE CAULFIELD AND ADAM DEROSE, FROM CRONKITE NEWS, SEPTEMBER 29, 2016

WASHINGTON – A 24-hour news cycle. Social media giving newsmakers a direct connection to the public that can bypass the press. The blending of political pundits and reporters analyzing day-to-day political dramas.

Americans consume news much differently in 2016 than they did when families gathered around the television to hear Walter Cronkite explain "the way it is" on the CBS Evening News.

Confidence in the media "to report the news fully, accurately and fairly" is at an all-time low, according to a September Gallup poll that found less than a third of Americans have "a great deal" or "fair amount" of confidence in the industry. Those were the lowest marks for media since Gallup began asking the question in 1972.

As media consumption changes, the industry faces obstacles that weren't envisioned when Cronkite manned the desk, said experts at a Newseum event Thursday celebrating the 100th anniversary of the newsman's birth.

"Back when Cronkite was at his height of his popularity there were only three networks," said Sharon Shahid, the Newseum's director of editorial content for video and interactive. "Now there are four networks and cable outlets and news is broadcast over so many different platforms … and that's not even including, Facebook, Twitter and all the other social media platforms."

It's unclear if America's relationship to its newsmen and women will continue to decline or if another transcendent figure will emerge, but Newseum visitors Thursday said they hope another iconic figure would one day command the attention of the nation.

"I don't think he's ever been matched," Shahid said. "He was the most trusted man in America back then – not the most trusted anchorperson, the most trusted man."

That history was lost on Maryam Majid, an 18-year-old who was visiting the Newseum with her classmates from Rock Ridge High School in Northern Virginia.

Majid, who is an editor of her school's paper, said she has never heard people her age mention Cronkite's legacy. But she wondered if current apparent biases in media coverage would make it harder for all Americans to agree on trusting the same person.

"I think that it would be nice to have someone that everyone would look up to, but it kind of just depends on what people want, and if the person actually supports their viewpoints," Majid said.

Another Newseum visitor said the distrust of the media might be linked to the larger divide in the nation.

"I think the country is so politically polarized, I don't know if it's because of journalism or if journalism has becomes polarized because of the mood in the country," said Peter Rosen, an anesthesiologist from Los Angeles.

1. The authors touch upon potential political biases in the news media. Can you think of other news coverage, other than political, that could suffer from media bias?

2. One person interviewed for the story raises a question: Is the country's political climate driving media bias, or is media bias causing the polarization? What do you think?

"PLEASE DON'T SHOOT THE MODERATORS," BY DONALD KAUL, FROM OTHERWORDS, NOVEMBER 4, 2015

We were treated to a classic man-bites-dog moment at the latest Republican presidential debate.

There the moderators were, CNBC's finest, lying in ambush with their carefully crafted "when did you stop beating your wife" questions at the ready. But as soon as they tried asking them, the contestants — forgive me, candidates — counter-attacked.

"How dare you ask me to explain my positions, you biased liberal media hack" was the general theme. And it worked. The crowd, a conservative group, roared its approval again and again.

The media is liberal, they say. It's biased against conservatives and it makes things up. A God-fearing, free-enterprise-worshipping American can't expect a fair shake from them.

Those are the inaccurate messages that went out, and I'm afraid that a frightening number of people bought it.

It's frightening because once the public assumes that the media is dealing from a stacked deck and can't be trusted, it loses faith in the very people, the only people, who can protect it from the lies of lying politicians. Lord knows the press does a lousy enough job of sorting out those lies anyway, but to remove the shield journalists offer altogether is unimaginable.

Besides, the CNBC-broadcast debate was replete with examples of the moderators letting the candidates get away with murder.

Ask Senator Marco Rubio, who seems to have become the favorite of pundits everywhere, any question of substance, and he takes you directly to the hardships suffered by his father the bartender and his mother the cleaning lady.

His jujitsu act was particularly impressive when he was asked about his appalling record in managing his personal finances.

Rubio dismissed the charges of over-spending, over-borrowing, and generally getting in over his head, and quickly played the "I didn't inherit a million dollars" card — followed by a return to the story of his father the bartender. It was game, set, and match. And we still don't know how a guy who can't balance his checkbook can hope to balance the federal budget.

The crew who did the questioning has taken a fearful beating from post-debate analysts, some of it deserved, some of it not.

The questioners were faced with a difficult task: how to get the candidates to stop dodging legitimate questions. In trying I thought they occasionally crossed the line between penetrating and snarky but — hey — it's television. You were expecting good taste?

Every GOP debate features some candidate or another complaining about liberal media bias. But it was left to Senator Ted Cruz to blow the CNBC panel out of the water.

He picked off four or five questions that had been asked, mischaracterized them a bit, and compared them with the softer questions Democrats were asked at their debate. It wasn't true, but it was a brilliant riff. The interrogators were left looking guilty, like students who'd been caught cheating on an exam.

He ended by stating that he doubted that any of the journalists there were going to vote Republican any time soon. It was the kind of remark that had the sense of a closing argument at a trial. The journalists never recovered.

The format of these so-called debates doesn't allow any space for the moderators to defend themselves from attack by a candidate. If it did, and if I were a brave highly paid network journalist on the panel, I would have said:

"Listen Senator, it's none of your business whom I vote for. That's why it's called a secret ballot.

"But I'm not here to be your best friend. I'm trying to get you to reconcile the inconsistencies in your record and your policies so that voters can figure out who you are and what kind of president you might be. So far, my colleagues and I have been unsuccessful, but we keep trying.

"In the meantime, if you would just answer the damn questions, we'd get along fine."

That probably wouldn't change things much, but it would sure make me feel a lot better.

1. As the author expresses, there's a strong belief that there is a liberal media bias and that the majority of news organizations and journalists favor liberal or Democratic candidates over conservative or Republican candidates. Do you think this is true? Explain.

2. The job of a debate moderator is to ask hard questions and get candidates to reveal the truth about their positions on various issues. Do you think the kind of "gotcha" tactics moderators often use could be considered an example of bias? Why or why not?

CONCLUSION

As long as the media is made up of people who have different views and ideas, there are likely going to be accusations that one source or another is biased in some way. As you read, these biases aren't always blatant; something as simple as using the phrase "illegal immigrant" instead of "refugee" or "migrant" can signal a bias. Bias can also be expressed through the interview subjects an outlet chooses to work with and the experts they depend on for information and analysis. But bias can also be expressed in more obvious fashion. It can be in showing only a small part of an event to avoid showing the whole truth, or it can involve misleading the audience through facts and figures—as certain politicians believe has happened in recent times. But as you read in chapter three, bias can include choosing how to present a story—and this is completely permissible, if not moral.

Still, journalists and media activists continue to watch the ever-changing media landscape to try to get back to the ideal of total objectivity. While many people believe this is a long-shot—as you explored in chapter one—the media will always have a role in society, and though most news consumers you talk to would say they would like to trust the media, it is unlikely that the media landscape will change unless the political landscape changes.

As you continue to read and watch and listen to the news, you'll need to use the things you've learned about media bias to help determine which stories you can trust in order to be a responsible news consumer.

BIBLIOGRAPHY

Baroud, Ramzy. "Navigating War: Has the War in Syria Also Destroyed Journalism?" Common Dreams, December 15, 2016. http://www.commondreams.org/views/2016/12/15/navigating-war-has-war-syria-also-destroyed-journalism.

Beaudoux, Virginia García. "Five Ways the Media Hurts Female Politicians—And How Journalists Everywhere Can Do Better." The Conversation, January 18, 2017. https://theconversation.com/five-ways-the-media-hurts-female-politicians-and-how-journalists-everywhere-can-do-better-70771.

Bolton, Matt. "Media Bias and the 'News' Form: A Historical Critique." Novara Media, March 27, 2016. http://novaramedia.com/2016/03/27/media-bias-and-the-news-form-a-historical-critique.

Born, Kelly. "The Effects of Fact-Checking." William & Flora Hewlett Foundation, April 28, 2015. http://www.hewlett.org/the-effects-of-fact-checking.

Buchler, Justin. "Does Nonpartisan Journalism Have a Future?" The Conversation, January 5, 2016. https://theconversation.com/does-nonpartisan-journalism-have-a-future-70384.

Caulfield, Claire, and Adam DeRose. "Election Coverage Reflects Fractured Media Landscape, Experts Say." Cronkite News, September 29, 2016. https://cronkitenews.azpbs.org/2016/09/29/election-coverage-reflects-fractured-media-landscape-experts-say.

Committee to Protect Journalists Staff. "Supreme Court Tells Argentina to Avoid Bias in Allocating Ads." Committee to Protect Journalists, March 4, 2011. https://cpj.org/2011/03/supreme-court-urges-argentina-to-avoid-bias-in-all.php.

Cope, Sophia. "Senator's Inquiry into Facebook's Editorial Decisions Runs Afoul of the First Amendment." Electronic Frontier Foundation, May 18, 2016. https://www.eff.org/deeplinks/2016/05/senators-inquiry-facebooks-editorial-decisions-runs-afoul-first-amendment.

Cushion, Stephen. "The Trumpification of the US Media: Why Chasing News Values Distorts Politics." The Conversation, March 10, 2016. https://theconversation.com/the-trumpification-of-the-us-media-why-chasing-news-values-distorts-politics-56033.

Downie, Andrew. "In Brazil, Journalists Face Injury from Violent Protests and Accusations of Bias." Committee to Protect Journalists, September 20, 2016. https://cpj.org/blog/2016/09/in-brazil-journalists-face-injury-from-violent-pro.php.

Flavio, Amando. "Mainstream Media Bias: Al Jazeera Blocks Article Criticizing Saudi Arabia For Human Rights Violations."

Anonymous Headquarters, December 27, 2015. http://anonhq
.com/mainstream-media-bias-al-jazeera-blocks-article-criticiz-
ing-saudi-arabia-human-rights-violations.

Forsling, Carl. "Americans Are to Blame for the Fractured State
of the Media." Task & Purpose, October 5, 2016. http://taskand-
purpose.com/americans-blame-fractured-state-media.

Glance, David. "Asking Users to Tag Fake News Isn't Going to Work
If They Don't Know What It Is." The Conversation, November 22,
2016. https://theconversation.com/asking-users-to-tag-fake-news-
isnt-going-to-work-if-they-dont-know-what-it-is-69268.

Gonsalves, Sean. "Understanding 'Media Bias." Common Dreams,
June 17, 2008. http://www.commondreams.org/views/2008/06/17/
understanding-media-bias.

Hollar, Julie. "I Play an Objective Expert on TV." OtherWords, March
1, 2010. http://otherwords.org/i_play_an_objective_expert_on_tv.

Inhofe, James M. "Criminalizing Forgery of Federal Documents."
United States Senate, September 28, 2004. http://www.inhofe
.senate.gov/newsroom/speech/criminalizing-forgery-of
-federal-documents-senate-floor.

International Media Support Staff. "Political Bias Saturates Egypt's
Media." International Media Support, August 20, 2013. https://
www.mediasupport.org/political-bias-saturates-egypts-media.

Kaul, Donald. "Please Don't Shoot the Moderators." OtherWords,
November 4, 2015. https://otherwords.org/please-dont-shoot
-the-moderators.

McClennen, Sophia A. "Can a Russian-funded Cable Network Actually Promote Free Press in the U.S.?" The Conversation, March 29,
2016. https://theconversation.com/can-a-russian-funded-cable
-network-actually-promote-free-press-in-the-u-s-54620.

Mutsvairo, Bruce. "Why Journalistic 'Balance' Is Failing the Public." The Conversation, November 25, 2016. https://theconversa-
tion.com/why-journalistic-balance-is-failing-the-public-68783.

New World Communications of Tampa, Inc., d/b/a WTVT-TV, Appellant, v. Jane Akre, Appellee. District Court of Appeal of Florida,
Second District, February 14, 2003. http://www.2dca.org
/opinions/Opinion_Pages/Opinion_Page_2003/February
/February%2014,%202003/2D01-529.pdf.

New World Communications of Tampa, Inc., d/b/a WTVT-TV, Appellant, v. Jane Akre, Appellee. District Court of Appeal of Florida,
Second District, February 25, 2004. http://www.2dca.org
/opinions/Opinion_Pages/Opinion_Page_2004/February/
February%2025,%202004/2D01-529.pdf.

Radical Centrist. "Political Bias and Perception." ThoughtUndermined.com, November 11, 2010. http://thoughtundermined.com/2010/11/12/political-bias-and-perception.

"Remarks by President Trump in African American History Month Listening Session." White House, February 1, 2017. https://www.whitehouse.gov/the-press-office/2017/02/01/remarks-president-trump-african-american-history-month-listening-session.

Salles, Alice. "Time Magazine's Latest Cover Story Is Full on Propaganda." The Anti-Media, October 7, 2016. http://theanti-media.org/time-magazine-clinton-propaganda.

Salzman, Jason. "The Truth's Liberal Tilt." OtherWords, May 21, 2012. http://otherwords.org/the_truths_liberal_bias.

Simon, Steven N. "Statement of Steven N. Simon — Senate Committee on Homeland Security and Governmental Affairs." United States Senate, September 12, 2006. https://www.hsgac.senate.gov/download/091206simon.

Spicer, Sean. "Statement by Press Secretary Sean Spicer." White House, January 21, 2017. https://www.whitehouse.gov/the-press-office/2017/01/21/statement-press-secretary-sean-spicer.

Taylor, Charlotte. "Migrant or Refugee? Why It Matters Which Word You Choose." The Conversation, September 14, 2015. https://theconversation.com/migrant-or-refugee-why-it-matters-which-word-you-choose-47227.

United States Congress. *Intelligence Authorization Act for Fiscal Year 2017*. 114th Cong., 2nd sess., H.R. 6393, 2017. https://www.congress.gov/bill/114th-congress/house-bill/6393.

United States Supreme Court. *Red Lion Broadcasting Co., Inc. v. Federal Communications Commission* (395 U.S. 367). 1969.

The University of Cambridge. "'Psychologiscal Vaccine' Could Help Immunise Public Against 'Fake News' On Climate Change — Study." January 23, 2017. http://www.cam.ac.uk/research/news/psychological-vaccine-could-help-immunise-public-against-fake-news-on-climate-change-study.

Webb, Whitney. "House Passes Bill Targeting 'Russian Propaganda' and 'Fake News.'" True Activist, December 4, 2016. http://www.trueactivist.com/house-passes-bill-targeting-russian-propaganda-and-fake-news.

CHAPTER NOTES

CHAPTER 3: WHAT THE COURTS SAY

NEW WORLD COMMUNICATIONS OF TAMPA, INC., D/B/A WTVT-TV, APPELLANT, V. JANE AKRE, APPELLEE, FROM THE DISTRICT COURT OF APPEAL OF FLORIDA, SECOND DISTRICT, FEBRUARY 25, 2004

1. We are aware of the Fourth District's decision in Forum v. Boca Burger, Inc., 788 So.2d 1055 (Fla. 4th DCA 2001), review granted, 817 So.2d 844 (Fla.2002). We have concluded that it is not pertinent to our decision because Salter still represents this district's position regarding whether defense of a judgment on appeal can ever be considered frivolous. Additionally, we find nothing in Forum that expressly repudiates that principle, which was the law in the Fourth District when Forum was decided. See Coral Springs Roofing Co. v. Campagna, 528 So.2d 557 (Fla. 4th DCA 1988). Rather, the holding in Forum is directed to the proper construction of a 1999 amendment to section 57.105, Florida Statutes, that the Fourth District concluded broadened the circumstances under which a fee award could be made under that statute.

RED LION BROADCASTING CO., INC. V. FCC, 395 U.S. 367 (1969) FROM THE UNITED STATES SUPREME COURT

1. Communications Act of 1934, Tit. III, 48 Stat. 1081, as amended, 47 U.S.C. § 301 et seq. Section 315 now reads:

   "315. Candidates for public office; facilities; rules."

   "(a) If any licensee shall permit any person who is a legally qualified candidate for any public office to use a broadcasting station, he shall afford equal opportunities to all other such candidates for that office in the use of such broadcasting station: Provided, That such licensee shall

have no power of censorship over the material broadcast under the provisions of this section. No obligation is
imposed upon any licensee to allow the use of its station
by any such candidate. Appearance by a legally qualified
candidate on any --"

"(1) bona fide newscast,"

"(2) bona fide news interview,"

"(3) bona fide news documentary (if the appearance of the
candidate is incidental to the presentation of the subject or
subjects covered by the news documentary), or"

"(4) on-the-spot coverage of bona fide news events
(including but not limited to political conventions and
activities incidental thereto),"

"shall not be deemed to be use of a broadcasting station
within the meaning of this subsection. Nothing in the
foregoing sentence shall be construed as relieving broadcasters, in connection with the presentation of newscasts,
news interviews, news documentaries, and on-the-spot
coverage of news events, from the obligation imposed upon
them under this chapter to operate in the public interest
and to afford reasonable opportunity for the discussion of
conflicting views on issues of public importance."

"(b) The charges made for the use of any broadcasting
station for any of the purposes set forth in this section
shall not exceed the charges made for comparable use of
such station for other purposes."

"(c) The Commission shall prescribe appropriate rules and
regulations to carry out the provisions of this section."

2. According to the record, Hargis asserted that his broadcast
included the following statement:

"Now, this paperback book by Fred J. Cook is entitled,
'GOLDWATER -- EXTREMIST ON THE RIGHT.' Who is
Cook? Cook was fired from the New York World Telegram
after he made a false charge publicly on television against
an unnamed official of the New York City government. New

York publishers and NEWSWEEK Magazine for December
7, 1959, showed that Fred Cook and his pal, Eugene Gleason,
had made up the whole story, and this confession was made
to New York District Attorney, Frank Hogan. After losing his
job, Cook went to work for the left-wing publication THE
NATION, one of the most scurrilous publications of the left
which has championed many communist causes over many
years. Its editor, Carry McWilliams, has been affiliated with
many communist enterprises, scores of which have been
cited as subversive by the Attorney General of the U.S. or by
other government agencies. . . . Now, among other things Fred
Cook wrote for THE NATION was an article absolving Alger
Hiss of any wrongdoing . . . ; there was a 208-page attack on
the FBI and J. Edgar Hoover; another attack by Mr. Cook was
on the Central Intelligence Agency . . . ; now this is the man
who wrote the book to smear and destroy Barry Goldwater
called 'Barry Goldwater -- Extremist Of The Right.'"

3. The Court of Appeals initially dismissed the petition for want of
a reviewable order, later reversing itself en banc upon argument by the Government that the FCC rule used here, which
permits it to issue "a declaratory ruling terminating a controversy or removing uncertainty," 47 CFR § 312, was, in fact,
justified by the Administrative Procedure Act. That Act permits
an adjudicating agency, "in its sound discretion, with like effect
as in the case of other orders, to issue a declaratory order to
terminate a controversy or remove uncertainty." § 5, 60 Stat.
239, 5 U.S.C. § 1004(d). In this case, the FCC could have determined the question of Red Lion's liability to a cease and desist
order or license revocation, 47 U.S.C. § 312, for failure to comply with the license's condition that the station be operated
"in the public interest," or for failure to obey a requirement
of operation in the public interest implicit in the ability of the
FCC to revoke licenses for conditions justifying the denial
of an initial license, 47 U.S.C. § 312(a)(2), and the statutory
requirement that the public interest be served in granting and
renewing licenses, 47 U.S.C. §§ 307(a), (d). Since the FCC could
have adjudicated these questions it could, under the Administrative Procedure Act, have issued a declaratory order in the
course of its adjudication which would have been subject to
judicial review. Although the FCC did not comply with all of
the formalities for an adjudicative proceeding in this case, the

petitioner itself adopted as its own the Government's position that this was a reviewable order, waiving any objection it might have had to the procedure of the adjudication.

4. Because of this chaos, a series of National Radio Conferences was held between 1922 and 1925, at which it was resolved that regulation of the radio spectrum by the Federal Government was essential, and that regulatory power should be utilized to ensure that allocation of this limited resource would be made only to those who would serve the public interest. The 1923 Conference expressed the opinion that the Radio Communications Act of 1912, 37 Stat. 302, conferred upon the Secretary of Commerce the power to regulate frequencies and hours of operation, but when Secretary Hoover sought to implement this claimed power by penalizing the Zenith Radio Corporation for operating on an unauthorized frequency, the 1912 Act was held not to permit enforcement. *United States v. Zenith Radio Corporation*, 12 F.2d 614 (D.C.N.D.Ill.1926). *Cf. Hoover v. Intercity Radio Co.*, 52 App.D.C. 339, 286 F. 1003 (1923) (Secretary had no power to deny licenses, but was empowered to assign frequencies). An opinion issued by the Attorney General at Hoover's request confirmed the impotence of the Secretary under the 1912 Act. 35 Op.Atty.Gen. 126 (1926). Hoover thereafter appealed to the radio industry to regulate itself, but his appeal went largely unheeded. *See generally* L. Schmeckebier, The Federal Radio Commission 1-14 (1932).

5. Congressman White, a sponsor of the bill enacted as the Radio Act of 1927, commented upon the need for new legislation:

"We have reached the definite conclusion that the right of all our people to enjoy this means of communication can be preserved only by the repudiation of the idea underlying the 1912 law that anyone who will may transmit and by the assertion in its stead of the doctrine that the right of the public to service is superior to the right of any individual. . . . The recent radio conference met this issue squarely. It recognized that, in the present state of scientific development, there must be a limitation upon the number of broadcasting stations, and it recommended that licenses should be issued only to those stations whose operation would render a benefit to the public, are necessary in the public interest, or would contribute to the development of the art. This principle was approved by every witness before your committee. We have written it into the bill. If enacted into law, the broadcasting privilege will not be a right of selfishness. It will rest upon an assurance of public interest to be served."

67 Cong.Rec. 5479.

6. Radio Act of 1927, § 4, 44 Stat. 1163. *See generally* Davis, The Radio Act of 1927, 13 Va.L.Rev. 611 (1927).

7. As early as 1930, Senator Dill expressed the view that the Federal Radio Commission had the power to make regulations requiring a licensee to afford an opportunity for presentation of the other side on "public questions." Hearings before the Senate Committee on Interstate Commerce on S. 6, 71st Cong., 2d Sess., 1616 (1930):

"Senator DILL. Then you are suggesting that the provision of the statute that now requires a station to give equal opportunity to candidates for office shall be applied to all public questions?"

"Commissioner ROBINSON. Of course, I think, in the legal concept, the law requires it now. I do not see that there is any need to legislate about it. It will evolve one of these days. Somebody will go into court and say, 'I am entitled to this opportunity,' and he will get it."

"Senator DILL. Has the Commission considered the question of making regulations requiring the stations to do that?"

"Commissioner ROBINSON. Oh, no."

"Senator DILL. It would be within the power of the commission, I think, to make regulations on that subject."

8. *Federal Housing Administration v. Darlington, Inc.*, 358 U. S. 84, 358 U. S. 90 (1958); *Glidden Co. v. Zdanok*, 370 U. S. 530, 370 U. S. 541 (1962) (opinion of MR. JUSTICE HARLAN, joined by MR. JUSTICE BRENNAN and MR. JUSTICE STEWART). This principle is a venerable one. *Alexander v. Alexandria*, 5

Cranch 1 (1809); *United States v. Freeman*, 3 How. 556 (1845); *Stockdale v. The Insurance Companies*, 20 Wall. 323 (1874).

9. *Zemel v. Rusk*, 381 U. S. 1, 381 U. S. 11-12 (1965); *Udall v. Tallman*, 380 U. S. 1, 380 U. S. 16-18 (1965); *Commissioner v. Sternberger's Estate*, 348 U. S. 187, 348 U. S. 199 (1955); *Hastings & D. R. Co. v. Whitney*, 132 U. S. 357, 132 U. S. 366 (1889); *United States v. Burlington & Missouri River R. Co.*, 98 U. S. 334, 98 U. S. 341 (1879); *United States v. Alexander*, 12 Wall. 177, 79 U. S. 179-181 (1871); *Surgett v. Lapice*, 8 How. 48, 49 U. S. 68 (1850).

10. *Zemel v. Rusk*, 381 U. S. 1, 381 U. S. 11-12 (1965); *United States v. Bergh*, 352 U. S. 40, 352 U. S. 46-47 (1956); *Alstate Construction Co. v. Durkin*, 345 U. S. 13, 345 U. S. 16-17 (1953); *Costanzo v. Tillinghast*, 287 U. S. 341, 287 U. S. 345 (1932).

11. An attempt to limit sharply the FCC's power to interfere with programming practices failed to emerge from Committee in 1943. S. 814, 78th Cong., 1st Sess. (1943). *See* Hearings on S. 814 before the Senate Committee on Interstate Commerce, 78th Cong., 1st Sess. (1943). Also, attempts specifically to enact the doctrine failed in the Radio Act of 1927, 67 Cong.Rec. 12505 (1926) (agreeing to amendment proposed by Senator Dill eliminating coverage of "question affecting the public"), and a similar proposal in the Communications Act of 1934 was accepted by the Senate, 78 Cong.Rec. 8854 (1934); see S.Rep. No. 781, 73d Cong., 2d Sess., 8 (1934), but was not included in the bill reported by the House Committee, see H.R.Rep. No. 1850, 73d Cong., 2d Sess. (1934). The attempt which came nearest success was a bill, H.R. 7716, 72d Cong., 1st Sess. (1932), passed by Congress but pocket-vetoed by the President in 1933, which would have extended "equal opportunities" whenever a public question was to be voted on at an election or by a government agency. H.R.Rep. No. 2106, 72d Cong., 2d Sess., 6 (1933). In any event, unsuccessful attempts at legislation are not the best of guides to legislative intent. *Fogarty v. United States*, 340 U. S. 8, 340 U. S. 13-14 (1950); *United States v. United Mine Workers*, 330 U. S. 258, 330 U. S. 281-282 (1947). A review of some of the legislative history over the years, drawing a somewhat different conclusion, is found in Staff Study of the House Committee on Interstate and Foreign Commerce, Legislative History of the Fairness Doctrine, 90th Cong., 2d Sess.

(Comm.Print.1968). This inconclusive history was, of course, superseded by the specific statutory language added in 1959.

12. "§ 326. Censorship."
"Nothing in this chapter shall be understood or construed to give the Commission the power of censorship over the radio communications or signals transmitted by any radio station, and no regulation or condition shall be promulgated or fixed by the Commission which shall interfere with the right of free speech by means of radio communication."

13. John P. Crommelin, 19 P & F Radio Reg. 1392 (1960).

14. The Proxmire amendment read:

"[B]ut nothing in this sentence shall be construed as changing the basic intent of Congress with respect to the provisions of this act, which recognizes that television and radio frequencies are in the public domain, that the license to operate in such frequencies requires operation in the public interest, and that, in newscasts, news interviews, news documentaries, on-the-spot coverage of news events, and panel discussions, all sides of public controversies shall be given as equal an opportunity to be heard as is practically possible."

105 Cong.Rec. 14457.

15. The general problems raised by a technology which supplants atomized, relatively informal communication with mass media as a prime source of national cohesion and news were discussed at considerable length by Zechariah Chafee in Government and Mass Communications (1947). Debate on the particular implications of this view for the broadcasting industry has continued unabated. A compendium of views appears in Freedom and Responsibility in Broadcasting (J. Coons ed.) (1961). *See also* Kalven, Broadcasting, Public Policy and the First Amendment, 10 J.Law & Econ. 15 (1967); M. Ernst, The First Freedom 125-180 (1946); T. Robinson, Radio Networks and the Federal Government, especially at 75-87 (1943). The considerations which the newest technology brings to bear on the particular problem of this litigation are concisely explored by Louis Jaffe in The Fairness Doctrine, Equal Time, Reply to Personal Attacks, and the Local Service

Obligation; Implications of Technological Change, Printed for Special Subcommittee on Investigations of the House Committee on Interstate and Foreign Commerce (1968).

16. The range of controls which have in fact, been imposed over the last 40 years, without giving rise to successful constitutional challenge in this Court, is discussed in W. Emery, Broadcasting and Government: Responsibilities and Regulations (1961); Note, Regulation of Program Content by the FCC, 77 Harv.L.Rev. 701 (1964).

17. This has not prevented vigorous argument from developing on the constitutionality of the ancillary FCC doctrines. *Compare* Barrow, The Equal Opportunities and Fairness Doctrines in Broadcasting: Pillars in the Forum of Democracy, 37 U.Cin.L.Rev. 447 (1968), with Robinson, The FCC and the First Amendment: Observations on 40 Years of Radio and Television Regulation, 52 Minn.L.Rev. 67 (1967), and Sullivan, Editorials and Controversy: The Broadcaster's Dilemma, 32 Geo. Wash.L.Rev. 719 (1964).

18. The expression of views opposing those which broadcasters permit to be aired in the first place need not be confined solely to the broadcasters themselves as proxies.
"Nor is it enough that he should hear the arguments of adversaries from his own teachers, presented as they state them, and accompanied by what they offer as refutations. That is not the way to do justice to the arguments, or bring them into real contact with his own mind. He must be able to hear them from persons who actually believe them; who defend them in earnest, and do their very utmost for them."
J. Mill, On Liberty 32 (R. McCallum ed.1947).

19. The President of the Columbia Broadcasting System has recently declared that, despite the Government,

"we are determined to continue covering controversial issues as a public service, and exercising our own independent news judgment and enterprise. I, for one, refuse to allow that judgment and enterprise to be affected by official intimidation."

F. Stanton, Keynote Address, Sigma Delta Chi National Convention, Atlanta, Georgia, November 21, 1968. Problems of news coverage from the broadcaster's viewpoint are surveyed in W. Wood, Electronic Journalism (1967).

20. Current discussions of the frequency allocation problem appear in Telecommunication Science Panel, Commerce Technical Advisory Board, U.S. Dept. of Commerce, Electromagnetic Spectrum Utilization -- The Silent Crisis (1966); Joint Technical Advisory Committee, Institute of Electrical and Electronics Engineers and Electronic Industries Assn., Report on Radio Spectrum Utilization (1964); Note, The Crisis in Electromagnetic Frequency Spectrum Allocation, 53 Iowa L.Rev. 437 (1967). A recently released study is the Final Report of the President's Task Force on Communications Policy (1968).

21. *Bendix Aviation Corp. v. FCC*, 106 U.S.App.D.C. 304, 272 F.2d 533 (1959), cert. denied, 361 U.S. 965 (1960).

22. 1968 FCC Annual Report 65-69.

23. New limitations on these users, who can also lay claim to First Amendment protection, were sustained against First Amendment attack with the comment, "Here is truly a situation where, if everybody could say anything, many could say nothing." *Lafayette Radio Electronics Corp. v. United States*, 345 F.2d 278, 281 (1965). *Accord, California Citizens Band Assn. v. United States*, 375 F.2d 43 (C.A. 9th Cir.), *cert. denied*, 389 U.S. 844 (1967).

24. *Kessler v. FCC*, 117 U.S. App.D.C. 130, 326 F.2d 673 (1963).

25. In a table prepared by the FCC on the basis of statistics current as of August 31, 1968, VHF and UHF channels allocated to and those available in the top 100 market areas for television are set forth:

COMMERCIAL

Channels

On the Air,

Channels Authorized, or Available

Market Areas Allocated Applied for Channels

VHF UHF VHF UHF VHF UHF

Top 10. . . . . . 40 45 40 44 0 1

Top 50. . . . . . 157 163 157 136 0 27

Top 100 . . . . . 264 297 264 213 0 84

NONCOMMERCIAL

Channels

On the Air,

Channels Authorized, or Available

Market Areas Allocated Applied for Channels

VHF UHF VHF UHF VHF UHF

Top 10. . . . . . 7 17 7 16 0 1

Top 50. . . . . . 21 79 20 47 1 32

Top 100 . . . . . 35 138 34 69 1 69

1968 FCC Annual Report 132-135.

26. *RTNDA* argues that these regulations should be held invalid for failure of the FCC to make specific findings in the rulemaking proceeding relating to these factual questions. Presumably the fairness doctrine and the personal attack decisions themselves, such as Red Lion, should fall for the same reason. But this argument ignores the fact that these regulations are no more than the detailed specification of certain consequences of longstanding rules, the need for which was recognized by the Congress on the factual predicate of scarcity made plain in 1927, recognized by this Court in the 1943 *National Broadcasting Co.* case, and reaffirmed by the Congress as recently as 1959.

"If the number of radio and television stations were not limited by available frequencies, the committee would have no hesitation in removing completely the present provision regarding equal time and urge the right of each broadcaster to follow his own conscience. . . . However, broadcast frequencies are limited, and, therefore, they have been necessarily considered a public trust."

S.Rep. No. 562, 86th Cong., 1st Sess., 8-9 (1959). In light of this history; the opportunity which the broadcasters have had to address the FCC and show that somehow the situation had radically changed, undercutting the validity of the congressional judgment, and their failure to adduce any convincing evidence of that, in the record here, we cannot consider the absence of more detailed findings below to be determinative.

27. The "airwaves [need not] be filled at the earliest possible moment in all circumstances without due regard for these important factors." *Community Broadcasting Co. v. FCC*, 107 U.S.App.D.C. 95, 105, 274 F.2d 753, 763 (1960). Accord, enforcing the fairness doctrine, *Office of Communication of the United Church of Christ v. FCC*, 123 U.S.App.D.C. 328, 343, 359 F.2d 994, 1009 (1966).

28. We need not deal with the argument that, even if there is no longer a technological scarcity of frequencies limiting the number of broadcasters, there nevertheless is an economic scarcity in the sense that the Commission could or does limit entry to the broadcasting market on economic grounds and license no more stations than the market will support. Hence, it is said, the fairness doctrine or its equivalent is essential to satisfy the claims of those excluded and of the public generally. A related argument, which we also put aside, is that, quite apart from scarcity of frequencies, technological or economic, Congress does not abridge freedom of speech or press by legislation directly or indirectly multiplying the voices and views presented to the public through time sharing, fairness doctrines, or other devices which limit or dissipate the power of those who sit astride the channels of communication with the general public. *Cf. Citizen Publishing Co. v. United States*, 394 U. S. 131 (1969).

GLOSSARY

angle—The approach a journalist uses when telling a story and the emphasis that is put on certain facts to convey the message the journalist wants to get across.

bias—Displaying favoritism to one side of an argument or story.

broadcast—Media that is transmitted through audio or video, as opposed to printed words.

conservative—Leaning to the right of the political spectrum. In most instances, it refers to those who support the thinking of the Republican Party.

editorial—An editorial is the official opinion of a media outlet. It is clearly identified as opinion and should not be considered part of a publication's news coverage.

Federal Communications Commission (FCC)—An agency of the US government that regulates communications by radio, television, wire, cable, and satellite in the United States and its territories.

GOP—An abbreviation for Grand Old Party, another name for the Republican Party.

left—When discussing politics or media bias, it refers to those who are aligned most closely with the Democratic Party. Frequently used interchangeably with "liberal."

liberal—Leaning to the left of the political spectrum. In most instances, it refers to those who support the thinking of the Democratic Party.

mainstream media—News outlets that are considered the most accessible and popular. Examples include the *New York Times*, Fox News, CNN, and other outlets that you would consider household names.

media—The collective term for any and all organizations or outlets that produce journalistic works.

objective—Being fair to both sides of a story and expressing no opinion.

press briefing—A meeting between the press secretary and the assigned White House correspondents in which the press secretary reads an official statement and may or may not take questions from attending journalists.

press secretary—The official spokesperson of the White House and the administration who speaks on behalf of the office of the president.

right—When discussing politics or media bias, it refers to those who are aligned most closely with the Republican Party. Frequently used interchangeably with "conservative."

subjective—Being influenced by personal feelings and showing a bias.

watchdog—An organization or person that monitors the media and reports on any instances of improper or unfair journalism.

FOR MORE INFORMATION

Atkins, Larry. *Skewed: A Critical Thinker's Guide to Media Bias*. Amherst, NY: Prometheus Books, 2016.

Falk, Erica. *Women for President: Media Bias in Eight Campaigns*. Champaign, IL: University of Illinois Press, 2008.

Goldberg, Bernard. *Bias: A CBS Insider Exposes How the Media Distort the News*. Washington, DC: Regnery Publishing, 2002.

Kuypers, Jim A. *Partisan Journalism: A History of Media Bias in the United States*. Lanham, MD: Rowan & Littlefield, 2014.

Levitin, Daniel J. *Weaponized Lies: How to Think Critically in the Post-Truth Era*. New York, NY: Dutton, 2016.

Niven, David. *Tilt? The Search for Media Bias*. Westport, CT: Praeger Publishers, 2002.

WEBSITES

Columbia Journalism Review
www.cjr.org
Since 1961, the *Columbia Journalism Review*, produced by the graduate school of journalism at Columbia University, has covered the media, discussing journalistic ethics and trends, and analyzing issues that face working journalists. It is considered one of the most respected sources of media criticism, and it frequently discusses how journalists can be better and avoid media bias in their reporting.

Fairness & Accuracy in Reporting (FAIR)
www.fair.org
FAIR has been working since 1986 to report on censorship and media bias. The organization believes that more diversity in journalism will help prevent bias and that the public has a role in alerting media outlets to their bias. By working with journalists and activists, FAIR is able to look at media bias from various angles and suggest ways in which the outlets accused of bias can improve their reporting.

CRITICAL PERSPECTIVES ON MEDIA BIAS

Media Matters for America

www.mediamatters.org

The first web-native media watchdog organization, Media Matters monitors print, online, television, and radio journalism for misinformation and offers immediate response and corrections through its online home and social media outlets. Although Media Matters focuses on conservative media bias, it produces long-form analyses and research papers that help journalists as well as news consumers find the bias in their news and combat it.

INDEX

ABOUT THE EDITOR

Jennifer Peters is a writer and editor whose work has focused on everything from relationships to book reviews to military and defense issues. During her more than ten years working in the media, her work has appeared in a number of magazines and online news and culture sites, with her most recent bylines appearing on VICE News and Task & Purpose. She lives in New York City, and she never leaves home without a good book.